THE DAMAGES LOTTERY

THE DAMAGES LOTTERY

——

P. S. ATIYAH

Formerly Professor of English Law
University of Oxford

·HART·
PUBLISHING

OXFORD

Hart Publishing
Oxford
UK

Published in the United States by Hart Publishing

© Patrick Selim Atiyah 1997

First published 1997. Reprinted 2000

Hart Publishing is a specialist legal publisher based in Oxford,
England. To order further copies of this book or to request a list
of other publications please write to:

Hart Publishing, Salter's Boatyard, Folly Bridge, Abingdon Road,
Oxford OX1 4LB. Tel. +44 (0)1865 245533. Fax (0)1865 794882
e-mail: mail@hartpub.co.uk

Payment may be made by cheque payable to 'Hart Publishing Ltd,
or by credit card.

British Library Cataloguing in Publication Data
Data Available
ISBN 1-901362-05-1 (cloth)
1-901362-06-X (cloth)

Typeset in 12pt Bembo
by SetAll, Abingdon
Printed in Great Britain on acid-free paper
by Biddles Ltd, www.biddles.co.uk

TABLE OF CONTENTS

PREFACE

THIS book is designed for the ordinary reader who may, perhaps, have read accounts of strange cases in which huge damages have been awarded for bizarre events, and wonders whether the law has gone mad. It is written in non-technical language and requires no previous knowledge of the law or the legal system. For the same reason it is not stuffed with learned references and lengthy footnotes. That does not mean that the facts and statistics presented here have been plucked out of the air — they are all capable of being documented and come from reputable scholarly sources or government publications. Anybody who seeks this documentation will find most of it in the author's *Accidents, Compensation and the Law*, the fifth edition of which, by Mr Peter Cane, was published in 1993 by Butterworth & Co. Although the present book has not been written for lawyers, some of them may find material here which will probably provoke them, and may even cause them to think more seriously about the issues discussed.

Some readers (especially those who may themselves have been involved in claims for damages) may feel that this book displays a lack of sympathy and compassion for accident victims. I entirely accept that sympathy and compassion have their proper place, but that place is in personal relationships. Those who care for the accident victim, even public officials like police and doctors, must provide their services with due regard for the emotional needs of accident victims. But legal and social structures, which deal with hard cash, must be subjected to rational discussion from time to time, and that kind of discussion is hindered rather than helped by emotional responses. It is that sort of rational approach which is offered in this book.

I am grateful to Peter Cane and Jane Stapleton for many helpful suggestions, and thanks are also due to my son Julian for the diagram in Chapter 4, and above all to Christine for giving me her reactions to the first draft in the capacity of 'ordinary reader'.

P.S. Atiyah

1. SUING FOR DAMAGES

IN 1995–96 two stories were reported in the national press. The first was about a man who slipped on a dance floor and fractured his leg. It was quite a bad injury which caused him some pain, and he was off work for several months, though in the end he made a full recovery. The dance hall was owned by the local authority and the injured man obtained over £10,000 in damages against them (which was in effect an award against the public taxpayers) because he was able to prove that the floor had been over polished and was hence too slippery. The second story was about a little girl of five years of age who was taken to hospital with a severe attack of meningitis. The doctors saved her life, but in order to do so they had to amputate both her legs. She had no chance of obtaining damages from anybody because her injuries were nobody's fault. It was just bad luck.

This book is largely about the different responses of the law to these two cases. They are not, of course, unique. There are many injured and disabled or handicapped people in our society. Some are unfortunate enough to be born with disabilities or handicaps; others suffer disabilities or injuries in accidents, others suffer disabling diseases or other conditions. There are also many accidental deaths, and many premature deaths from natural causes. Most of these people are entitled to some benefit or other from the social security system; some get assistance from local authorities' social service departments. But a tiny handful receive large damages under the system of civil liability – what lawyers call the law of torts. Who are the few who receive such damages? Why do they get such generous treatment compared to the thousands of others who suffer similar injuries or handicaps? Who is actually paying for the damages? How fair is the system? How efficient is it?

In recent years actions for damages for injuries, real or imagined, appear to have become far more common. Levels of damages, for some cases at least, are far higher than they were a few years ago – in the most serious cases of personal injury, damages may now be of the order of a million pounds or more. New types of cases are constantly being recognised by the courts, especially claims for post-traumatic stress and other psychological conditions. Over the past fifty years the law has been stretched in many directions – in nearly every case the stretching is favourable to plaintiffs by enlarging the number of cases in which damages can be awarded, or by improving the levels of damages. The stretching is still going on, though some judges are at last beginning to resist the attempt to enlarge legal liability still further at the frontiers. Complaints are often heard that we "are going down the American road" without, very often, explaining what the American road is, and what is wrong with it. But what is increasingly obvious is that the present system is as unjust and inefficient as it could be. A lot of people – especially lawyers – think the present system is unjust because too few people are entitled to damages, and they get too little. They think accident victims are badly treated by the legal system. This book has been written in the conviction that the truth is precisely the reverse of this. The system is indeed unjust, but for quite different reasons. Many of the wrong people get compensated, they get too much and the wrong people pay for it – in fact, the public pays for it, but not in fair shares. The system is not only unjust, but also exceedingly costly and inefficient, and this has been proved time and again by research studies all over the world.

This book attempts to explain to the concerned citizen

some of the issues involved, gives a brief account of the law, and discusses what has gone wrong. In the concluding chapter some suggestions are offered for a completely new approach to the problems of compensation for personal injury. Although the details are complex, in its essentials the subject is straightforward and not difficult to understand even for those with no knowledge of the law, or the legal system.

THE LAW OF NEGLIGENCE

I start with a very brief account of the law of negligence. The first thing that must be grasped is that the law of damages, or more accurately, the law of civil liability, is not generally designed to *punish* anyone. Punishment is the function of the criminal law; compensation is the function of the civil law. The possibility of punishing those guilty of causing injuries is dealt with more fully in Chapter 7, but for the moment we will concentrate on the compensation question.

In very straightforward cases the law of negligence is really perfectly simple. In general terms the law provides that any person who is injured by the *fault* of another can claim damages for those injuries. Lawyers call the complaining or suing party the plaintiff, and the person who is being sued, the defendant, and it will be convenient to stick with these words. In simple cases there is nothing esoteric about the legal concept of fault – lawyers define it as a failure to take reasonable care according to all the circumstances of the case. In the case of road accidents, with which most people are familiar, the concept of negligence includes such simple faults as driving too fast in the conditions, overtaking on a dangerous corner or bend, failing to keep a proper look-out for other road users, and so on. What is more, in simple cases like this, most people would find the law not only quite straightforward and intelligible, but also entirely fair. If we put aside injury cases for the moment and consider a simple case where one person's vehicle is damaged by the fault of another driver, not many people would disagree with the fairness of the law which says that in these circumstances the person at fault should pay for the damage done. People may, of course disagree strongly about *who* actually was at fault in a particular situation, but where the element of fault is quite clear, very few people would find it unfair that the guilty party should pay for the damage. For example, where a person damages a car by carelessly reversing into it in a car park, there is not much room for argument over whose fault the accident is, and in a case like this, where the damage is likely to be quite modest, a reasonable motorist would readily agree that the guilty party should pay – even where he is himself the guilty party. The existence of insurance is a complicating factor, which will have to be considered at length later, but in a very simple case like this, insurance is often disregarded by both motorists for very good reasons, and the justice of requiring the guilty driver to pay would generally be unquestioned.

The law only requires *reasonable care* – it does not require all possible care, nor does it generally impose legal liability where damage or injury is caused by pure accident. For example, staying for the moment with road accidents, which are likely to be within the experience of many people, a driver who causes an accident because he is stricken with a sudden incapacitating heart attack may be acquitted of negligence, because the accident simply was not his fault. He may have caused the accident, but he has not necessarily been guilty of a lack of reasonable care. But that assumes that the heart attack has come suddenly and without warning. A reasonable driver who feels seriously ill while driving, and is aware, or ought reasonably to be aware, that he may be unable to control the vehicle properly, ought perhaps to pull over and wait until he feels better. If he carries on regardless, he may be guilty of negligence. Notice how I say that the driver *may* be, rather than that he *is* guilty of negligence in such circumstances. That is because negligence must be looked at according to *all the circumstances of the case*. So, for instance, whether a driver who feels ill ought to pull over and rest, or is justified in carrying on, may depend on a whole range of factors – how ill does he feel, is he aware that he may have heart disease, what are the road conditions at the time, what kind of road is he on (motorway or country lane?), does he have good reasons for wishing to press on, and so on.

On the other hand, although the law only requires reasonable care, it is no defence for a driver to say that he was doing his best. His best may simply not be good enough. Drivers do not have to display the abilities and skill of a Damon Hill or a Michael Schumacher, but they must display the abilities of the ordinary reasonably careful driver. And a driver who is simply unable to do this, because he just is a bad driver, or even because he has a physical disability, will be guilty of negligence just the same.

It must be stressed that negligence is a very minor kind of fault, in the legal sense. All sorts of acts may be held to be negligent by lawyers which are only marginally blameworthy – a doctor, for instance, fails to ask a patient whether he is allergic to penicillin, or an employer fails to provide his workers with earmuffs when they are engaged in noisy work which may over a long period damage their hearing. Although negligence can sometimes be followed by devastating consequences (for example, serious injury or even death), and the lay public may for that reason tend to think that some serious fault has occurred, lawyers insist – and rightly insist – that consequences like this are often more or less accidental, for example because they were not really foreseeable. A minor act of negligence is not made more morally culpable because, by mischance, it leads to very serious injuries to another person. Nor must we think that, because a defendant is held to have committed some act of negligence, he has necessarily done something which would be morally blameworthy.

STRICT LIABILITY

In addition to liability for negligence, lawyers recognise another form of liability which they call "strict liability". In these cases it is not necessary to prove negligence at all in order to claim damages, but it is relatively unusual to be able to claim damages for injury in a strict liability case. There are two kinds of cases in which such a claim may be made which could be of relevance for our purposes.

First, a person who can sue for damages for breach of contract may not have to prove negligence, so if you buy dangerous or defective goods (which is in law a contract) you can claim damages from the seller, not merely for the value of the goods themselves (or the cost of repairing them) but also for any any damage done *by* the goods. So if, for instance, you buy a new washing machine which is, say, electrically faulty, and it blows up throwing water all over your kitchen, destroying the clothes in it, and perhaps injuring you into the bargain, you can claim damages for all these things. You will not need to prove the seller was negligent; it is sufficient that the goods you have bought are faulty within the definitions laid down in the Sale of Goods Act. And these definitions are very wide indeed. Similarly, if you buy infected meat from a butcher, and the meat poisons you, it is not necessary to prove it was the butcher's fault that the meat was infected, because buying meat is a contract of sale of goods just as much as buying a washing machine.

Second, there are other cases where you may sometimes be able to claim damages for defective goods under the Consumer Protection Act 1987, without proof of negligence. As against the seller this is not very important because your rights under the Sale of Goods Act are so extensive; but if you want to sue the manufacturer or importer (rather than the seller), or if a member of your family is injured and wants to sue someone, it may not be possible to claim under the Sale of Goods Act. In this case it is sometimes possible to sue under the Consumer Protection Act, and again negligence is not needed. But you will still have to show that the goods were "defective" and in practice this kind of strict liability will not often add a great deal to your right to sue for negligence.

A consumer's right to claim damages for faulty goods is of course an important part of the law, but his right to sue for damage done *by* faulty goods is less important, and in this book I shall in general ignore these possible strict liability claims for damages. Statistically speaking they are of very minor importance compared to the great mass of claims for damages for negligence.

INTENTIONAL TORTS

Naturally, the civil law provides redress for intentional wrongdoing as well as in cases of negligence and strict liability. So there are obvious torts like assault and wrongful arrest (strictly, false imprisonment), though here too the "stretching" process goes on, and the judges have recently recognised harassment as a new intentional tort, which may well prove an important "growth" area of the law. In general this book is not concerned with these intentional torts, and certainly no proposal will be found here to abolish or reduce the liability of a person who commits an intentional tort. But there are some cases which do raise issues with intentional torts which are really identical to issues which arise with negligence, and which are discussed more fully later. These cases concern the liability of employers or others for the actions of a wrongdoer. When, for instance, a policeman uses excessive force in arresting someone (and thereby commits a tort) the police authority will be liable for the damages, just as much as the policeman himself. This kind of liability – which is actually the liability of the public in the last resort – is very much the concern of this book, and raises problems in no way different from the liability of police officers for negligence. But apart from that this book is not concerned with intentional torts which do not give rise to anything like the volume of claims and litigation which negligence does.

LIABILITY FOR HOW MUCH?

Lawyers commonly keep quite separate two important questions. The first is the question of *liability*, which is largely dependent on the proof of negligence, as already explained; the second is the question of what damages are to be awarded. But when the fairness or justice of the law is being examined many people might find it odd to separate these two questions. Surely, most people would say, whether the law is fair depends not only on whether a defendant is held liable, but on *how much* he is liable for? The reason that lawyers do not generally perceive this is probably because they take the basic principle of the law of damages to be entirely self-evident and reasonable: the defendant is liable to pay whatever sum of money is necessary to put the plaintiff back in the position, so far as money can do it, in which he would have been if there had been no negligence, no injury at all. In very simple cases of damage to property (such as the road accident which damages a car but causes no injury) this principle works perfectly easily. The defendant has to pay the cost of repairing the damaged car, or if it has to be written off altogether, the market value of the car.

But in cases of personal injury, and in fatal cases, the basic principle has to be supplemented by so many further rules, that things get a lot more complicated. At the moment we will try to concentrate on the essentials, leaving further details to be elaborated later.

Injury cases: financial losses

In injury cases the damages to which the plaintiff is entitled fall into two categories. First, there are damages to cover the plaintiff's money losses. For instance the plaintiff may have been off-work for a few weeks and so lost wages of so many hundred pounds. These are recoverable in full as part of the damages. This means that high earners will recover much larger damages than low earners, or those who are not employed at all. The higher your earnings, the more your losses will be if you are deprived of them. Monica Seles, the tennis star, is currently suing for some £10 million for her lost earnings as a result of being stabbed by a deranged spectator at a German tennis tournament, though she has lost the first legal round of her claim. A QC who suffers a minor injury and so misses a single court appearance may lose several thousand pounds, and can recover the whole lot in damages (less tax). A labourer might recover only £50 for his lost earnings for that period; a housewife not gainfully employed will not recover anything for loss of earnings because she has lost none, and the same is true of an unemployed person. (On the other hand, it is also true that some highly paid employees will actually suffer little or no loss of earnings for short-term incapacities, because their employers will continue to pay their salaries for a few weeks' or even months' of absence, where a lower paid employee may actually lose his pay.)

The plaintiff is not, however, limited to claiming for past lost earnings – if he suffers a long-term injury he will be able to claim for estimated future losses, and it is these future losses which often inflate the damages into very large figures. Naturally, when a young person suffers a permanent injury, and is compensated for loss of earnings for his whole working life, the damages may be enormous. Even if he was not earning at all when injured, because (for instance) he was then unemployed, or was still a student who had not begun to work, he may be able to recover for future earnings losses, because he might have had reasonable expectations of securing some employment in the future.

If the plaintiff is so badly injured that he will never work again, everything that he might have earned in the future is treated as a "loss", so it will be necessary to estimate the entire loss of earnings throughout his life in order to calculate the damages. This is often a difficult business: where the plaintiff suffers his injury at a relatively young age it is necessary to predict what would have happened to him if he had not been injured – would he, for example, have been promoted, would he have had a successful professional career, or in the case of a woman, would she have married and had children, or would she have remained in employment throughout her life, and so on. It is even necessary to estimate how much the plaintiff might have earned by way of pension – years before he has reached retiring age. Obviously all these questions can only be answered with rough and ready estimates – "guesstimates", perhaps. In theory judges are supposed to make allowance for the fact that they are indeed making estimates about uncertain possibilities, so the damages are discounted (reduced) because even if the plaintiff had not been injured in this accident he might in the future have anyhow had periods of unemployment or sickness. One does wonder, though, whether these discounts adequately reflect the possibility that work prospects in our society may themselves be changing quite radically.

Where the plaintiff's injuries are really serious – where he is, for instance, permanently paralysed or bedridden – it is obviously necessary that he should have an income from some source or other, throughout his life, and it is hardly surprising that if he is entitled to damages, they will cover his whole working life. But today judges often seem to be very generous in assuming that other less serious injuries will render the plaintiff permanently unemployable. There are, for instance, many claims for post-traumatic stress these days in which relatively young people are declared by doctors to be incapable of working again, and judges accept these findings, apparently without question. In 1996 a case of this kind came before the Court of Appeal in which over £1.3 million had been awarded but the plaintiff had made an almost complete recovery within a few months. Because the facts came to light before the court's final order was drawn up the damages were substantially reduced as a result – but if the facts had come to light only a few months later, the plaintiff would probably have kept the whole lot.

When a person suffers injuries or shock of this kind, he can respond in one of three ways. He may, first, make every effort to rehabilitate himself, to overcome his handicaps, and try to fit himself so far as he can for a job, and as normal a life as possible. Not every injury prevents a person working – after all there are many disabled people who manage to lead useful and fulfilling lives – there are blind and deaf members of parliament, for instance. Other blind people have had very successful careers as academics or in other walks of life. Douglas Bader became a famous acepilot in the war despite having lost both legs in a pre-war accident. Franklin Roosevelt served as President of the United States for over twelve years, though crippled by polio and unable to walk unaided. Not everybody can be a Bader or a Roosevelt, but many disabled people, forced to use wheelchairs for their transport, are vigorous in their demands that working opportunities should be opened for them. It is paradoxical, and undesirable, that when a claim for damages is pending, such people should be told that they cannot be expected to work again.

Faced with this sort of response, it is not surprising if the victim responds to his injuries in quite a different way. He may simply assume that he can never lead a normal life again, never work again, and make no effort to rehabilitate himself. A third possibility is that an injured person may decide that he cannot hope to recover while his claim for damages is pending, and may prefer to get that settled before he decides what to do with his life.

A major problem with the law at present is that it penalises the person who reacts in the first way described above, and rewards anybody who responds in the second or third way. In these respects the law clearly sends out the wrong messages to accident victims. It positively invites them to exaggerate their symptoms, to make no effort to rehabilitate themselves before their claims are settled. Those who manage to find some useful employment will only recover damages for the difference between what they can now earn and what they might have earned if they had not been injured. Those who can persuade the judge that they can never work again will receive the highest damages – though once they are awarded the plaintiff is not prevented from then trying to find useful work to do. It may well be that the severity of the recent recession, with high unemployment rates, has resulted in an increase in the levels of damages, as those who are seriously injured are likely to have more difficulty in finding work when they have recovered, and may also find it easier to persuade judges that they will never work again. Of course judges who have to decide whether an injured victim is likely to be able to work again have to base their decisions on the evidence, and doctors seem as much to blame for the present state of affairs as judges. They appear far too willing to tell a serious injury victim that he has no chance of ever working again, and to encourage the victim to believe just that.

It is unhappily true that the disincentive effects of compensation systems are not confined to cases in which damages are claimed. Social security and private insurance systems may also suffer to some degree from the same problem, but the situation is greatly aggravated by the fact that damages are usually paid in a single lump sum.

In addition to losses of earnings, there may be all kinds of medical and even social costs to be estimated as well. Despite the existence of the NHS an injured person is entitled to seek private medical and hospital treatment, and have all the costs (and estimated future costs) paid for by the defendant as part of the damages. This right extends to nursing care, too. For instance the plaintiff, if so seriously injured that he is likely to remain bedridden, may be entitled to claim the estimated cost of private nursing care throughout his life (for 24 hours a day, in the most serious cases). Then there are what may be called social costs. A housewife who is injured may be able to recover the cost of employing someone to do her work while she is out of action, even though she cannot recover for lost earnings. In other cases there may be additional costs such as the adaptation or even the purchase of a specially suitable house, a car, and other amenities. Damages to cover these expenses are often awarded on the most generous basis, which it may seem mean to question given the very serious injuries which the plaintiff may have suffered. Yet it has to be remembered constantly that many others who suffer equally (or even more) devastating injuries, not caused by anybody's fault, receive no damages at all. When this is borne in mind, the extreme generosity displayed by the law to plaintiffs who are entitled to damages seems more questionable.

In principle these claims to financial losses are simple: the plaintiff is entitled to be compensated for every penny of his financial losses, once it is understood that all future losses are also included in this term. In practice, of course, the process often requires difficult estimates to be made. In addition, there is the further complication that whenever an estimate is made of future financial loss, but the damages are to be paid at once, the total figure must be discounted, that is reduced, to reflect the fact that the plaintiff is going to receive it now, and obviously a lump sum today is worth more than a future income which would have been received over many years. The method of discounting these future financial losses is complex and controversial, but the details need not concern us. What does need to be understood is that many of these difficulties stem from the fact that the damages are usually estimated and paid once for all. Under a different system, where the compensation is paid weekly, or monthly, it would be unnecessary to make these guesses about the future.

Injury cases: non-pecuniary loss

The second head under which the plaintiff is entitled to be compensated is for non-pecuniary losses – what are sometimes called damages for pain and suffering, or damages for loss of amenity. Lawyers take the view that the plaintiff would not be fully compensated if he did not receive something for the injury itself, over and above the financial losses he has suffered. In the most serious cases of all, where the plaintiff is permanently incapacitated – rendered a quadriplegic, for example, paralysed in all four limbs – simply replacing his financial losses does not come anywhere near to offering him genuine compensation. So the plaintiff is entitled to additional damages for these "non-pecuniary losses". Although sometimes called damages for pain and suffering, actual pain and suffering do not have to be proved. In fact these damages can be awarded (though usually at a somewhat lower rate) even to a plaintiff who is in a permanent vegetative state, and never recovers at all. For this reason judges now tend to call the damages for non-pecuniary loss awards for "loss of amenity".

Of course there is a serious problem about these damages for loss of amenity, because there is no way of putting any

real financial figure to them – there is no market value for
these "losses". This difficulty has been solved by the courts
by the adoption of a sort of tariff in which the most serious
injuries of all are given a value of (today) around £130,000,
while other injuries are then tested against this figure.
Nobody pretends that this is a completely satisfactory
method of solving the problem, but it has some advantages.
First, it is administratively workable, because the judges
and barristers and insurance administrators who operate the
system know the tariff and can usually predict fairly closely
the point on the scale where the plaintiff's case will fall. So,
although nobody can expect to predict the exact figure
which a judge is likely to award for non-pecuniary loss, an
experienced barrister can usually say that the case is likely
to fall within the range (say) of £10,000 to £15,000, or
perhaps of £60,000 to £70,000 in a more serious case. The
second advantage of the system is that it has a reasonable
internal consistency, in that the more serious injuries will
usually be compensated more generously. In general,
damages for non-pecuniary losses are no more for higher
earners than for lower earners.

Is the maximum figure for damages for non-pecuniary
loss too low at around £130,000? Many people probably
think it is, though it must be remembered that, in cases
where the maximum is likely to be awarded, the damages
for the pecuniary losses could easily be a million pounds or
more. English judges would agree that it is exceptionally
difficult to fix an actual figure for the highest levels of damages for non-pecuniary loss (from which figures for all less
serious cases are ultimately derived) but would argue that
there is simply no purpose in piling on the damages in these
cases. As a judge once said of an unfortunate girl who was
permanently paralysed and bed-ridden, in one sense all the
gold in the Bank of England would not really compensate
her for what had happened. There is simply no point in
awarding immense sums to injured people who will never

really get much benefit from them. Provided that their medical and other needs are met, and something can be done to let them enjoy their lives to the limits of their medical condition, still further payments serve no real purpose.

What is more, although it may seem callous to draw attention to the fact, it has to be faced that where the plaintiff is so badly injured that he is unable to use the compensation to any great degree, much of it is likely to pass to his heirs in due course, and frequently after no great length of time. Those who suffer the sort of terrible injuries which lead to the highest damages generally have a shortened expectation of life. To some degree this problem is now alleviated by the fact that in the worst cases of all the damages are often awarded by means of an annuity, which will of course come to an end when the plaintiff dies.

Although in very serious injury cases the damages for non-pecuniary loss will be a relatively small proportion of the total damages awarded, this is not generally true of less serious injury cases. Indeed, at the time of the Pearson Royal Commission Report in 1978 it was estimated that about two thirds of all damages were paid as compensation for non-pecuniary loss. This was much higher than most people thought, and it tends to confirm doubts about the utility of the whole system. Once it is understood that damages are not meant to punish the defendant, and that they will not actually be paid by the wrongdoer anyhow, it must be accepted that damages for non-pecuniary loss are in most cases plainly a lower priority than damages for pecuniary loss. It is clearly more important that the victim have an income, than that he has something extra for pain and suffering, especially for minor injuries. If you doubt this, ask yourself which risk you yourself would choose to insure against if you were buying the insurance and paying the premium – loss of your income, or pain and suffering? Yet a very large part of the cost of the whole system is actually devoted to funding these small claims for non-pecuniary loss.

Damages for non-pecuniary loss have probably declined over the last few decades as a proportion of the total damages awarded in injury cases, but the reason for this is that there has been a corresponding increase in damages for pecuniary loss. This has occurred because plaintiffs' lawyers nowadays try to think up every conceivable way in which an injured person may have suffered financial loss as a result of his injuries, and then claim for these losses. For example, a plaintiff who used to do – as most of us do – his own gardening, or home decorating and other DIY jobs round the house, may now claim he is unable to do these as a result of his injuries, and so has to pay someone else to do them. Very well – an estimate of these sums (past and future) now becomes a pecuniary loss which can be recovered by the plaintiff. Or again, the plaintiff now has to remain at home when before he went out to work, so in the winter his house has to be heated all day. So increased winter fuel bills become another item of financial loss, recoverable by the plaintiff.

The result is that damages for non-pecuniary loss may well be somewhat lower (allowing for inflation) than they used to be. They are certainly very far from American levels, where, as is well known, such damages often run into millions even for relatively minor injuries. This is certainly one road we have not gone down, and there is no likelihood that we will, because damages in America are usually fixed by juries and in England by judges. Juries are apt to be profligate with other people's money, and may not appreciate that they, in common with other members of the public must in the end pay for the damages they award through their insurance premiums and other payments. Some American insurance companies have tried to educate juries on these matters, even to the extent of handing out leaflets to potential jurors saying: "Higher verdicts mean higher premiums". That too is a road down which we are unlikely to travel in England.

All the elements of the damages are of course cumulative, so the plaintiff is entitled to the figure for his financial losses and his non-pecuniary losses, added together. In addition he is often entitled to interest on the totals because in serious cases it is often years before the money is paid.

Members of the public sometimes get an exaggerated idea of the amount of damages that can be claimed in minor cases. They read in the press of someone receiving £30,000 for being bullied in school and they may well think that this is an absurd amount of compensation for such a minor injury as being bullied. Or again, they may read of the plaintiff who was awarded £200,000 for post-traumatic stress following the death of his brother in the Hillsborough disaster.[1] This book argues that damages *are* often too high, but it must be understood that awards of this kind are likely to be based on the assumption that the plaintiff has suffered substantial losses of earnings. Figures like this are based on medical evidence suggesting that the plaintiff has been so traumatised that he has suffered a serious mental illness which has prevented him from working for some considerable time, or perhaps, will prevent him working again at all. In other words these damages are being awarded not *because* the plaintiff has been bullied or *because* he has lost his brother. They are awarded because the plaintiff has lost earnings (which will have to be demonstrated) as a result of the trauma following the bullying or the death of his brother.

Fatal cases

Fatal cases present special difficulty. They fall into two classes. First, there are cases falling under the Fatal Accidents Acts, where the plaintiff claims for the financial

---

[1] *The Times*, 12 December 1996, p. 9.

losses he (or more usually she) has suffered as a result of the death of someone on whom he may have been dependent. A wife who is being maintained by her husband, or a child maintained by a parent, is generally held to suffer financial losses when the spouse or parent is killed in an accident. That financial loss is recoverable against a negligent defendant in very much the same way that a living accident victim can recover for his financial loss. First it is necessary to estimate how much the deceased used to spend on the spouse or child, then to estimate for how long this dependency would probably have lasted, and then to make some global estimate, discounting the future loss because a capital sum is going to be awarded. As in the case of a living victim, the principle is relatively straightforward – the plaintiff is entitled to full compensation for every penny of financial loss – but obviously the precise quantification is often a bit of a rough estimate. Once again, the dependants of a high earner will receive much higher compensation than those of a lower earner. What is more, the young wife of a wealthy earner who is completely maintained by him will recover much higher damages than the young working wife who keeps herself and shares the bills with her husband.

The second class of case concerns the death of someone who has left no dependants (or probable future dependants). For instance, when a minor child is killed, or when an elderly retired person is killed, there will often be no financial loss to anyone. So in principle, nobody would be able to sue at all in this situation. But many people would find this logic too much to stomach, and the law does therefore make some provision for a very modest form of compensation for the death of an unmarried minor child, or of a spouse, which is in addition to any claim for financial loss. The amount to be awarded in this type of case is fixed by statute and is at present £7,500. Many people clearly find this sum extremely low as compensation for the shattering loss of a young child, and certainly in other legal systems, such as most of the United States, enormous awards of damages may be made for death in such a case.

But this is an American example which our law has so far not followed, and surely with good reason. What is the point of awarding large damages for the death of a small child? It will not bring the child back, and it can surely do nothing to assuage the grief which must be felt by the parents. It is natural to feel sympathy for the grieving parents who have lost their child in what may be a horrible accident, but what purpose is served by translating this sympathy into cold pounds? Once again, it must be accepted that not all the gold in the world would really compensate a parent for loss of a child. It seems very likely that what motivates parental demands for higher damages in such cases (if it is not distasteful gold-digging) is a desire to punish those they believe to be responsible for the accident. But as we have seen, the civil law is not concerned with punishment. If the responsible party has committed a crime, he can and should be prosecuted, and dealt with by the criminal courts, but requiring large damages to be paid will achieve nothing. It will achieve nothing because the damages will not actually be paid by the party responsible, but by his employer, or most likely by an insurance company. Once again, one can test the validity of these arguments by asking whether you would want to insure the life of your children if you were paying the premiums yourself. Surely most people would find the very idea repulsive (and it is actually illegal anyhow). Nobody wants financial compensation for the death of a child, looking at the possibilities in the future.

We shall see later (p. 56 ff.) that increasingly lawyers are finding a way round the limit of £7,500 which is recoverable by the parents of young children killed in accidents. What has been happening lately is that lawyers are persuading judges that the parents are entitled to damages *in their own right* for the trauma they have suffered (and its consequences) following the death of a child. In this way they may succeed in recovering vastly more than £7,500.

WHO PAYS?

Who pays these damages? That is actually quite a complex question which will be dealt with in some detail in Chapter 5, but it is such an important question, and it is so inter-related with the subject-matter of this and the next two chapters, that a few preliminary words must be said about it here. Although it is often difficult to say who exactly does (in the last analysis) pay for awards of damages, it is at any rate clear who does *not* pay them. The damages are hardly *ever* paid by the actual wrongdoer, the negligent party. They are usually paid, in the first instance, by insurance companies, or by public bodies like the government or trust hospitals. But insurance companies do not (as some people seem to think) just pay these sums out of "profits". They pay them out of premiums paid by the public, directly or indirectly. Ultimately, most damages are paid for by the public, very much as they pay taxes; that is, the cost is spread around fairly thinly. But as everybody knows, taxes add up, and so do damage awards. So the first thing to be grasped here is that any demand for more damages and higher damages must lead to higher premiums for the public. This is a vital point because much public and even legal commentary on the desirability of extending legal liability or awarding higher damages seems to assume that the damages fall from the sky. The fairness of the system of damages and the appropriate sums that should be paid in damages, are often discussed entirely without reference to the other side of the equation. Even the Law Commission (an independent body of expert lawyers with a general responsibility for law reform) whose proposals are usually well thought-out, is quite prepared to discuss the question whether damages for injury are too low without asking what the effect of increasing damages would be on insurance premiums. This is absurd. It is just like calling for higher social security benefits without asking what extra taxes will have to be raised to cover them. Most people today know that that kind of thing is irresponsible, but everybody should understand that calls for higher damages are equivalent to calls for higher insurance premiums and also (as we shall see) higher prices for goods and services.

SUING AND SETTLEMENTS

In order to understand, even in general terms, how the present system works, the reader needs to realise that most claimants who recover damages do not actually need to sue. Most claims – about ninety-nine percent in fact – are simply presented by a solicitor acting on behalf of the plaintiff, and are then bargained over between the solicitor and the insurance company representing the party responsible. Strictly speaking therefore there may never be an actual law suit, there is no suing, and the parties never actually become plaintiff and defendant, the terms appropriate to legal proceedings. But it is convenient to continue using these terms anyhow. Both parties are well aware that it is a lengthy and costly business actually to fight out a case in court, and so it is usually in the interests of the parties to "settle" the case out of court, if they can do so. In most cases, after a certain amount of correspondence and haggling between the parties or their representatives, the insurance company will make an offer to the plaintiff which he is willing to accept, and that will be the end of the case. So the plaintiff never actually has to go to court to give evidence.

The bargaining process in personal injury cases sometimes favours the insurance company rather than the plaintiff, particularly in very serious cases. Sometimes this happens simply because the insurers (and their lawyers) are much more experienced in handling cases of this kind than some solicitors acting for plaintiffs. Sometimes it happens because the plaintiff may be in rather desperate financial straits, and so may be willing to settle for less than he could expect to get if he held out for more. Sometimes it is because of an important rule about costs. Suppose the insurance company offers a definite sum to settle the case – say, £10,000 – and the plaintiff refuses the offer. If the case goes to trial, the plaintiff is indulging in a high risk strategy because even if he wins the action he will be ordered to pay a large part of the costs of the action if he is eventually awarded less than £10,000. This may swallow up most or even all of the damages, in which case the plaintiff won't actually receive anything at all – in fact he may even be left owing his solicitor a substantial debt. So the plaintiff is under great pressure to accept what may be offered.

On the other hand in less serious cases, the pressure to settle may be the other way. Every claim, no matter how trivial, has a nuisance value, and will cost the insurance company money to handle and process. So the temptation to pay off a small claim for a few hundred or even a few thousand pounds may be very great even though the insurance company may strongly suspect that the claim is largely a put-up job, with very little merit – for example, because they think the plaintiff was himself to blame for the accident. Or because they are very sceptical of his claim for financial losses, or to have had any real pain and suffering. What is more, many plaintiffs can easily obtain legal aid in these personal injury cases (provided only that they qualify under the means test), and in legal aid cases the plaintiff cannot be required to pay the defendant's costs if he loses his action. This means that the insurance company is often on a hiding to nothing in cases of this kind. Suppose their costs are likely to amount to at least £5,000 even for a fairly trivial case, which they probably will if the case goes to court. If the insurance company lose the case they will have to pay the plaintiff damages and his costs, as well as their own costs. If they win the case, they will still have to pay their own £5,000 worth of costs. If the plaintiff knows these facts (and his solicitor should explain them to him) he will appreciate that he himself stands to lose very little out of an exaggerated or even a wholly bogus claim. Not surprisingly, in a case like this, the insurance company may well feel obliged to try to settle the case by offering (say) £2,000 in damages.

Another factor which often explains why some apparently unmeritorious claim may be paid off with substantial damages in settlement, is that the claim may be typical of many others in the pipe-line, and the insurance company wants to avoid setting a precedent which may become very costly to it in the future. Two cases of this kind have recently been reported in the press. In the first a young person obtained £30,000 in settlement of a claim against a local authority school for injuries caused by prolonged bullying; and in the second a payment of £1,000 was made to a boy whose teeth were said to have been mottled by a well-known brand of toothpaste. It rather detracts from the insurance company's purpose if these cases are widely reported in the press because even though the settlement may not constitute a legal precedent, the publicity alone may well generate lots of new claims, so sometimes insurers only settle on condition that the amount paid is not disclosed. And if they know that there are a lot of claims which are definitely going to be pressed, then this may operate in precisely the reverse direction, that is to say the insurance company will be more likely to fight from the beginning rather than to settle.

There can also be other – perfectly praiseworthy – reasons why a defendant may prefer to settle. Suppose, for instance, that a trust hospital is being sued in a complicated negligence case. They may be confident that the plaintiff's chances of proving negligence against them are low, but to allow the case to go to trial may mean that many doctors and nurses employed by the hospital will be distracted for a prolonged period – for years, indeed – by the threat of the litigation and ultimately the trial itself. Endless detailed inquiries may need to be made, records searched, staff interviewed and so on – none of this is likely to be conducive to the hospital's main job of treating its patients. It is not surprising that hospitals prefer to settle claims against them.

One other thing needs to be said about the settlement process. In legal theory the plaintiff himself remains in charge of the procedure, and his solicitor is simply his agent who must do what he is told. So the plaintiff may at any time drop the case, or choose to accept whatever has been offered, contrary to his solicitor's advice. Quite often he can even insist on continuing with the case contrary to his solicitor's advice, although in an extreme case the solicitor may decide he will not continue to handle the claim. But in practice it may well be that many plaintiffs find it hard to reject the advice they are given, or to interfere very much in the process. This means that, once the case gets to a solicitor, the usual legal procedure tends to be followed. The solicitor will regard it as his duty to seek the best possible result for his client, and the client gets caught up in a process he does not understand. Of course it is the solicitor's duty to explain matters to his client, and to indicate the possible choices he may have, but there will be a strong tendency for the solicitor to assume that the client wants what the law expects him to want – namely to claim the damages to which he is legally entitled. So even if the client approaches a solicitor in the first instance with only a very hazy understanding of his rights or what he wants – he may for instance, not even be seeking damages, but rather wishing to punish a defendant – the case may in practice get out of his hands very quickly.

LEGAL AID, AND "NO WIN NO FEE" CASES

As everybody knows, going to law, or even going to lawyers, can be a pretty expensive business, but this does not in practice prevent poor people from making many kinds of claims for damages. In straightforward personal injury cases, where there seems a clear case of negligence, a solicitor will often be quite willing to try to negotiate a settlement for the plaintiff, without asking for any advance on his fees, in the confident expectation that his fees will eventually be paid by the defendant's insurance company.

In more complicated cases a solicitor may be unwilling to proceed unless the plaintiff can obtain legal aid, but for people of modest means this is relatively easy and painless – provided the plaintiff is poor enough and has a reasonable case in law, he will be entitled to legal aid. Paradoxically, middle income people will be worse off, because they may not qualify for legal aid (nearly half the country will not qualify) and may be seriously at risk if they proceed very far with a claim, although even then many cases are so clear-cut that some settlement is virtually certain.

Legal aid is now costing the taxpayers about one billion pounds a year, but civil claims for damages only account for a small part of this. Since most claims do result in some payment from the defendant's insurers, and it is the custom for insurers to pay the legal bill almost as a matter of course whenever a settlement is reached, the legal costs do not generally fall on the Legal Aid authority in the long run. They may have to fund a claim in its early stages, but ultimately the costs will be paid by the defendant's insurers and the Legal Aid authorities are then reimbursed. Only in the relatively rare cases where there is a complete victory for the defendant, is the Legal Aid authority left holding the bill for the plaintiff's lawyers. The Legal Aid authority is very keen to stress this fact so that the public should not think they – the public – are funding all these claims. But it must be understood that, even though most legal costs are paid for by the defendant's insurers, the public is still ultimately paying the bill, although they are paying as premium payers rather than as taxpayers. As we saw in the last section (p. 21) it is actually the public who pay most of the damages in the end, and they have to pay the costs too.

Recently lawyers have been permitted to take cases on a new basis – the "no win no fee" basis. A lawyer willing to take on a case on this basis is entitled to charge more if he does succeed in getting some compensation for his client; but if nothing is recovered the client is not at risk at all. These cases are similar to the American "contingent fee" cases which are often criticised by English lawyers, though Americans think they are an excellent way of ensuring that really poor people can get access to the courts. The main difference between the American practice and the new English practice is that in America the lawyer charges the client a percentage of the damages recovered – commonly forty percent. That is still not permitted in England, where the lawyer's fees must be proportionate to the work required of him, and not to the damages recovered.

What is not yet clear – though there are ominous signs – is whether the new English practice will bring in its train some of the undesirable results of the American contingent fee. These undesirable results flow from the fact that the client has absolutely nothing to lose by embarking on a claim, however exaggerated or bogus the claim may be, and some lawyers may find it worth taking on such claims because there is always the possibility that they may be able to get something by way of a settlement even in the most unpromising circumstances. Given how easy it is to get legal aid for most damages claims, it is only too likely that the ones taken on the "no win, no fee basis" will be the least promising cases where legal aid is refused. There is therefore a real possibility that this procedure may actually foment litigation. People who would not otherwise think

of suing or making a claim may be encouraged to do so.
Lawyers may not only find it worth taking on these sort of
claims, they may actually go out looking for them.

In extreme cases this can lead to the behaviour known in
America as "ambulance chasing", that is, having lawyers or
their touts pursuing injured people into hospitals and trying to persuade them while still lying injured in bed to sign
contracts for the lawyer to take up their claims for damages.
Lawyers do not indulge in this sort of thing in England, and
hopefully they never will. But less extreme forms of behaviour may be encouraged which still help to foment claims
or litigation – lawyers may, in other words, start advertising
for clients, and this can get pretty close to ambulance chasing, for example where the advertisements are posted up in
hospital casualty departments. In fact advertisements have
already begun to appear in England suggesting that if you
have been involved in an accident, or been injured somehow, the advertiser may be able to help you recover damages. In America advertisements are often even more
obviously designed to stir up litigation, for example, they
may say:

> Anxious? Depressed? Stressed?
> Is your employer treating you fairly?
> You may be entitled to compensation.
> All cases taken on contingent fee.

Naturally, this sort of advertising encourages litigation
and the attitude of mind that leads to claims being made,
even where the injured person would not otherwise have
thought of it at all. Lawyers tend to argue that this is not a
bad thing. If people have legal rights, they should be made
aware of them, and encouraged to pursue them. If others

have infringed their rights by negligence, it is a good thing (they say) if litigation against these wrongdoers is actually encouraged. But this seems facile. For one thing, as we shall have to emphasise over and over again, it is not the negligent wrongdoer who will pay the damages at all. And anyhow, if people do not feel seriously aggrieved, it does not seem desirable that they should actually be encouraged to feel aggrieved. It seems particularly undesirable that people should be encouraged to feel aggrieved, and to claim damages for their grievances, when they are also likely to be told that the more miserable and depressed they are, the more they are incapable of leading a normal life and getting back to work, the higher will be the damages they can recover. Litigation, and even making claims that can be easily settled, is also costly to society, and in the long run, the more of it there is, the more the cost to the public. We have seen, too, that negligence is often a very minor fault, and we should not think that it is objectionable that negligence should go unpunished or even uncorrected.

Although ambulance chasing by lawyers is unknown in England, there are today a number of people calling themselves "claims assessors" or "claims negotiators" whose practices sometimes come close to ambulance chasing. These people have no legal or other qualifications, though they are not prohibited from acting on behalf of claimants for damages. But anybody who uses their services is unlikely to obtain a satisfactory settlement because they are not entitled to issue proceedings on behalf of a client, nor even to recommend them to a solicitor.

The contingent fee, or the no win, no fee practice, may lead to entrepreneurial lawyers investing large sums of money in bringing on a whole series of similar cases, with all the planning and research that may be involved, even where there is very little justification for the claims at all. It is, for instance, well known in the US that there are several groups of lawyers at present engaged in three massive litigation battles, or campaigns, as it might be more accurate to call them, which have been going on for well over a decade. There are those involving litigation against tobacco companies on behalf of lung cancer and other victims of smoking; there are those involving similar litigation on behalf of many alcoholics (and their families) against the producers and importers of spirits and other liquor, and there is a third group who are the victims of shootings by hand guns who are suing the hand gun manufacturers. Very few of these claims would have much chance of success if they went to trial, for reasons which will become clearer during the course of this book, but they are still serious enough to involve the tobacco, alcohol and hand gun industries in massive legal expenditure; so a few strategic settlements may from time to time be necessary. At the end of the day, huge settlements have been made in some other cases of this kind, though when the amounts paid over are distributed to thousands of plaintiffs it has been found that they receive only a handful of dollars each while the lawyers collect several million dollars in fees.

Conditions in England are not quite the same, although here too there is now a considerable effort being put into the planning of some litigation against the tobacco companies. Legal aid has been withdrawn from these claimants because the legal aid authorities apparently no longer believe they have a reasonable case in law; but the solicitors involved are still pursuing them on the no win, no fee basis.

There have also been other similar mass-action campaigns arising from use of drugs or medical procedures later discovered to be, or claimed to be, defective or dangerous. Most of these claims originate in the US where the same drugs or procedures have been used, and spread to England when the publicity starts encouraging people to go to lawyers. Despite the immense effort and money put into some of these mass claims in America, very few of them have produced significant gains to the plaintiffs, or have even succeeded in proving that the drugs or procedures in question were faulty, or the cause of the conditions of which complaint was made. In fact in some cases these same medical procedures are still in use in England where doctors do not believe there is anything wrong with them, even after damages have been obtained in the US. In England one large mass claim financed by legal aid (rather than the no win, no fee basis), has recently been concluded. This case, concerning allegedly faulty tranquillisers, cost the Legal Aid authorities some £30 million in fees for lawyers (and expert consultants, medical drug advisers etc.) although at the end of the day all the actions were struck out before they even reached trial. This was certainly taxpayers' money down the drain.

2. HOW THE LAW HAS BEEN STRETCHED

IN simple cases, as we saw in the last chapter, the law looks perfectly fair and straightforward. A person who injures another as a result of negligence or fault should pay full compensation to the injured party. But we shall now look at a variety of ways in which the law has been stretched out of all recognition. In almost every situation, the stretching has been done in favour of injured accident victims.

The reader may wonder what is wrong with stretching the law in this way – perhaps this is the law actually being human, showing sympathy for victims. Unfortunately, stretching the law like this is not really a good idea, for reasons which will become apparent in the course of this book. The basic problem is that those who are compensated with damages are a tiny minority of all victims of accidents and disabilities, and the more we squeeze into this category, the less money is likely to be available for the great majority of these victims. It is rather as though, faced with a hundred homeless people living on the street, we picked out one or two and lodged them in the Ritz at our expense. If we then stretch things a little more here and a little more there, perhaps we could afford to help one or two more of the homeless and put them in the Ritz too. But we shall then find that the bill from the Ritz is so large that we shall have little or nothing to spend on the remaining 96 still sleeping on the street. So stretching things here will actually have made things worse.

STRETCHING THE CONCEPT OF FAULT

The first thing that has been stretched is the very concept of negligence itself. It must be repeated that negligence is not the same thing as *moral* fault – which is one of the reasons that negligent behaviour is often not criminal, but only gives rise to civil liability. People can easily commit acts of negligence without being in a moral sense personally to blame for what has happened. They may cause an accident for reasons of inexperience, or clumsiness or even basic incompetence. Obviously there are a lot of motorists on the road who are not very skilful drivers – the elderly, the excessively cautious, the timid, the learner drivers, those who have little experience of particularly bad conditions, such as heavy rain or night driving, and so on. The law does make some allowance for these things, but generally speaking, only in a broad brush sort of way. So, for instance, the law may indeed make some allowance for the fact that the weather conditions are very bad, so that a person cannot be expected to be able to stop his car as quickly when the road is icy as when conditions are good – but he must still drive as carefully as a reasonably skilled driver, even though he may never have encountered such conditions before himself. Or again, the law may distinguish between the skill of a medical GP and that of a consultant, so that a GP may not be negligent if he fails to spot a condition that a consultant ought to spot; but the law does not distinguish between the care and skill required of a GP just because he has only recently qualified. So a professional person can easily be held guilty of negligence even where he does not himself feel that he did anything wrong, even perhaps where he thinks he would do the same thing again.

Then again, the law often seems to mean that a person can never be allowed to make a mistake without being branded as negligent. Actually that is not quite correct.

Here too the law does sometimes make allowances. It recognises that in some circumstances even a reasonable man may make a mistake – where for instance, some disaster occurs, and instant decisions are required, but in the "agony of the moment" somebody makes the wrong choice. This may be held not to amount to negligence.

At the same time, people in all walks of life do often make mistakes – and they may well be mistakes which careful and prudent people *should* not make, so they will be held to amount to negligence. Yet who can be reasonably careful and prudent all the time? We all commit negligence, probably several times every few minutes when driving a car, and often when doing our work as well. Even the most dedicated and skilled professional people make mistakes which they should not make – even (perish the thought) barristers and judges do so. The finest sportsmen in the world constantly commit errors which the merest schoolboy might have avoided. Think, for example, of the professional footballer, who skies his shot over the bar when faced with an open goal, or the tennis champion who tamely nets his shot when his opponent's court is wide open. Luckily mistakes like this do not often cause anybody an injury so sportsmen do not find themselves accused of negligence for making them – though perhaps one day a Wimbledon ball boy will be injured by a wild shot and will claim compensation on the ground that the player was negligent.

Being wise after the event

As we all know, it is easy to be wise after the event, and some may feel that judges are prone to this temptation, branding as negligence conduct which seemed perfectly acceptable at the time. Actually, the law does recognise this danger, and it is quite clear as a matter of strict theory that judges are not supposed to decide that someone has been negligent in the light of subsequent events or subsequent knowledge. But some may feel that, despite this, judges do sometimes fall into the temptation of doing so. This is particularly liable to occur when the allegation of negligence does not turn upon some simple act like a piece of carelessness in driving on the road, but arises from much more complex situations – when it is suggested (for instance) that a company should have been aware that certain chemicals used in their plants carried a risk of long-term injury to the health of the workers in that plant. In modern times employers are expected to be well-versed in the literature of occupational risks arising from chemicals and other hazards like dust or asbestos or (still more obviously) radiation, and if they are not, they are certainly likely to be found to be negligent. But thirty or forty years ago many of these risks were much less well-known to employers, even though they were actually documented in scientific literature. The result is that (for example) many employers have recently been held liable for negligence for failing to take precautions to protect their workers from exposure to asbestos thirty years ago, and there does seem to be an element of being wise after the event about some of these decisions. The fact that asbestos was still being widely used, not merely by profit-seeking companies, but also by public authorities (including the Royal Navy) long after the scientific facts were known, will doubtless enrage those people who are convinced that all companies and all public bodies are invariably engaged in a conspiracy to do down the common man; but others may feel less sure about this. After all, public bodies are not out to make money, and the officials who authorised the use of materials which eventually turned out to be extremely dangerous did not personally gain from their conduct. So when we ask why they did it, the honest answer must often be, because everybody else was doing it, and the full extent of the risks was not really appreciated even though in an ideal world perhaps they should have been.

The stretching effect of sympathy

It will be seen that we encounter here a problem which, in one shape or another, lies at the heart of the mess into which the law has got. On the one hand, we feel sympathy for the injured person. And this sympathy is likely to be stirred all the more strongly if we have listened to a very detailed account, from medical witnesses, of the injuries he has received, have heard, for instance, about the fractures and pain that have been suffered, about the operations needed, about the likely future disability that the injured plaintiff may have to live with for years, about the fact that he is now unemployable, and so on. Lawyers and judges are human, and they do, in many cases, have to go through precisely this procedure. On the other hand, what about the defendant? Does anybody feel sorry for him? If he has not been morally at fault, but may possibly have fallen below the standard of care required by the law, it may seem hard to condemn him as negligent, and order him to pay many thousands of pounds (perhaps hundreds of thousands) in damages. But sympathy for the defendant is very rarely as great as sympathy for the plaintiff, and there are two reasons for this, one obvious, one less obvious. First, and most obviously, sympathy for the damage to the defendant's reputation is a small matter, in most cases, when weighed against sympathy for injury to life or limb. Occasionally, but only occasionally, the matter of the defendant's reputation may assume greater importance, especially when he is a doctor or surgeon, to whom the damage to his reputation may be especially wounding; and in these cases it may well be that the law is not so often stretched as it is in other cases.

But even in these cases, there is a second factor which makes sympathy for the plaintiff usually outweigh any anxieties we feel about the defendant. And this is – a point which we will have to return to again and again – that the defendant will not actually pay the damages even if he is found guilty of negligence. The damages will in almost every case be paid for by an insurance company, or an employer or other public body. So the lawyers and judges know perfectly well that an adverse finding of negligence against a defendant will not actually hurt him in any material respect, whereas an adverse finding against the plaintiff will deprive him of his chance of compensation. What is more, even in cases where the defendant's reputation may be a matter of great personal importance to him, as where he is a doctor or other skilled professional, the judge will know that an adverse finding of negligence is unlikely to have any serious consequences. After all, the doctor's employers, or partners, will know, or will be told, that a finding of negligence carries no necessary moral blame, and should not be taken as an imputation of general incompetence or lack of care, so it is unlikely that his career will suffer. In fact judges sometimes go out of their way, when recording a finding of negligence against a professional person, to make it clear that they intend no general reflection on the defendant's competence. So the defendant's *amour propre* may be hurt, but his pocket and his career are unlikely to be affected.

Some readers may wonder about my suggestion that the law can be "stretched" by sympathy. Surely, they may think, judges are supposed to be neutral and dispassionate enforcers of the law. Of course that is true, as a matter of theory. But judges are human, and can feel the tug of sympathy, like everybody else. When the facts of a case are quite clear, and when the law to be applied to those facts is also clear, no judge is likely to be false to his oath because of sympathy for one litigant rather than another. And we can also reject the preposterous slur on the judges (propagated by Auberon Waugh in the *Sunday Telegraph*[1]) that

---

[1] 24 November 1996.

they expand the law of liability because they are lawyers and more liability is good for the lawyers. But when the facts are not entirely clear, and still more, when the law is not wholly settled, there is room for judges to develop it in one direction or another. As we shall see, the development of the law has in the past fifty years or so been almost uniformly in the direction of expanding liability – more liability for more damages. And, as we shall also see, it is not only the judges who are to blame for these developments. Parliament, the Law Commission and perhaps even academics, may have a share of the responsibility.

STRETCHING THE LAW WHERE THE DEFENDANT IS NOT SOLELY TO BLAME

In many cases of accident or injury, the causes are complex, and more than one person may well be responsible. In many road accidents, for instance, it is the combined fault of two (or even more) drivers which produces the accident. What is to happen then? We will distinguish two situations – in the first, the plaintiff himself is partly to blame, and in the second there are two or more defendants who are all to blame.

If the plaintiff is partly to blame for his own injuries, the rule of the early common law was that he could not recover any damages at all. It did not matter that the defendant was more to blame – if the plaintiff had any share of the responsibility for the accident or the injuries, he could not recover at all. The plaintiff was said to be guilty of "contributory negligence". This often seemed unfair, and judges frequently stretched the law in a variety of ways to help an injured plaintiff. We need not go into these in any detail, because they are today obsolete. An Act passed by Parliament in 1945 says that where an injury is caused partly by the fault of the defendant, and partly by the plaintiff's own fault, the damages must now be apportioned according to the degree of fault of the parties. Of course translating fault into percentage terms cannot be done in any very precise arithmetic way, but in practice it does not seem to give judges much trouble. In a rough and ready way, it is often quite easy to say that the parties were (for instance) equally to blame, or that the defendant was perhaps seventy percent to blame while the plaintiff was thirty percent to blame. If the parties were equally to blame, that means that the plaintiff will recover half the compensation which would otherwise be awarded; if the defendant is held seventy percent to blame, that means that the plaintiff will only recover seventy percent of the damages which he would otherwise have got. So contributory negligence reduces the damages but does not deprive the plaintiff of all right to claim.

At first sight, this reform looks quite reasonable and fair, like the negligence principle itself. After all, if the defendant is partly responsible for the accident, why should he not pay for that partial responsibility? So long as we look solely at the two parties in the case, sheer justice seems to demand this result. But actually, a little thought will show that this reform was a far more profound change than was appreciated by Parliament who passed it, or the judges who implement it. To appreciate how profound a change it was, it is necessary to bring together two points. First, the new Act for the first time breached the principle that a person should not be compensated for injuries which were even partly his own fault; and secondly, we must remember that the compensation will not be paid by the guilty party himself, but by an insurance company or other broad section of the community. That means that the plaintiffs who are entitled to obtain compensation in civil liability claims can no longer be treated as an innocent group who, as a whole, deserve specially generous treatment at the hands of the public. After all, lots of people suffer injuries, accidents, disabling illnesses, congenital disabilities and so on. Very few of them obtain, or have any chance of obtaining, damages. At one time, those who did obtain damages could at least be seen to be a group who were quite free of responsibility for their injuries – even though that might also be said of many others who could not obtain damages. But now we see that many of those who do obtain damages *are* partly responsible for their own injuries, yet they are still more generously treated than many who have no entitlement to damages, and yet have no responsibility for their injuries at all.

What is more, it must be remembered that damages in serious cases can be very high indeed, even after a substantial reduction because of the plaintiff's own share of the responsibility for his contributory negligence. Take one casual example, drawn from the newspapers.[2] In November 1996 a young man of 24 was awarded £350,000 in damages for injuries received in a cycling accident eleven years earlier, when he was only 13. Despite his youth, the judge held that the boy was seventy percent responsible for his own injuries, otherwise he would have been awarded about £1.2 million. By chance, the damages in this case were awarded against the Ministry of Defence, because the vehicle involved was an army truck, and the negligent driver was an army employee. Damages awarded against the Ministry of Defence must, of course, be paid for by the public, the taxpayers. So this plaintiff who was seventy percent responsible for his own injuries was paid £350,000 in compensation by the public. Yet every year, many babies are born with very serious congenital deformities and disabilities, none of whom will ever receive any damages from the public. This does not seem fair or just.

Another case, also by chance against the Ministry of Defence, is perhaps even more offensive to normal ideas of justice. In this case (in 1995) the plaintiff's husband, a naval

[2] *Oxford Times*, 22 November 1996.

airman, drank himself into an alcoholic stupor, and then choked to death on his own vomit. The court decided that, although the Ministry was not, of course, responsible for the man's getting himself drunk, Ministry employees did see him when he was completely incapable of looking after himself, and failed to realise (as a reasonable person would have done) that a person in such a drunken condition might indeed choke on his own vomit, and should therefore have been monitored constantly. The man was held two thirds to blame for his own death, but that still left the widow with an award of over £70,000 in damages – about twenty times as much as the annual pension which a widow with young children would receive in social security benefits. But this widow would have been entitled to her social security benefits as well as the damages.

These may have been extreme cases, but road accidents constitute the main single source of compensation claims, and in a very high proportion of road accidents, the plaintiff is at least partly to blame for his injuries. So this means that a good proportion of those who obtain damages under the present law are partly responsible for their own injuries.

We mentioned above that there is a different set of rules applicable where the plaintiff was not himself to blame, but the defendant was only partly to blame. There are, in other words, several guilty defendants, or anyhow several parties responsible who could be held to be negligent. Now here too the law is "stretched" in favour of the plaintiff, though in rather a different way from the stretching in cases of contributory negligence. The stretching in these cases takes the form of allowing the plaintiff to choose which defendant or defendants he will sue, and permitting him to recover *all* the damages from any of them. (But he cannot recover more than he has lost by suing more than one defendant – he will still only recover once for his losses.) The defendants who are sued and made to pay can, in turn, recover a share of the damages from the other guilty parties. Again, it all sounds very fair on the surface. Why should the plaintiff be forced to worry about which defendant to sue? Why should he be involved in arguments over which defendant was responsible for how much of the damage? Why should they not fight that out themselves, leaving the plaintiff meanwhile to quit the fray, as it were?

But once again, the apparent fairness only exists on the surface. The real problem is that one or more of the defendants may be impecunious and uninsured, while others may be insured, or may be wealthy corporations or public bodies. When this is the case the plaintiff naturally claims all the damages from the defendants who can pay, leaving them to claim in turn against the defendants who can't pay. What is more, this remains the situation even if the defendant who can pay is only slightly responsible for the accident, while the one who can't pay was largely responsible. To illustrate – suppose an accident occurs which is the result of the combined negligence of a cyclist and a lorry driver, and a third party is injured in this accident. The third party will claim against the driver and recover *all* his damages from the driver's insurance company. The insurance company could in theory turn round and sue the cyclist for his share of the third party's damages. But a cyclist is very unlikely to be insured against that liability, so they would not recover any of the damages that way. And that would still be the case even if the cyclist was ninety percent responsible for the accident and the driver only ten percent responsible. In this kind of situation the judge will be under a great temptation to "stretch" the facts and find that the lorry driver was partly responsible even if only to the extent of ten percent or five percent. That is enough for the third party to recover all his damages.

The fact that you can claim *all* the damages from any person bearing *any* responsibility for the accident leads to a very important practical rule of thumb followed by all lawyers. This rule is, in effect, *cherchez l'argent* (as distin-

guished from *cherchez la femme*), or, search for a defendant
who can pay, rather than for the person who is most to
blame. Once you have found a possible defendant who can
pay (either because he is insured or because he – or it – is
a wealthy corporation, or a public body) then you can set
about trying to pin some share of the blame on that person. With a bit of ingenuity, it is surprising how easy it can
be to construct a case against a potential defendant even
though, on the face of it, his connection with the accident
was minimal. In fact accident victims sometimes think
nobody was really to blame for their injuries until a solicitor explains to them that somebody can be blamed for what
has happened, as a matter of law. To illustrate, suppose a
road accident is caused by a child running across the road
and causing a vehicle to swerve into another: here the child
seems the responsible party, but a child pedestrian would
not make a good defendant. But suppose the child was in
the care of some adult – perhaps a schoolteacher. Now we
are getting somewhere. Where there is a teacher, there
must be a school which employs the teacher, and a school
should make an excellent defendant. There are many other
situations in which this simple principle is at work. A person is injured in a rugby match. Tough luck, you may
think, rugby is a physical game. But perhaps the referee was
to blame – try suing him, rugby referees are insured. Or
again, a police driver chasing a car thief skids on some ice
and crashes into a lamp-post injuring himself, while the car
thief speeds away. The thief does not appear to have been
directly responsible for the policeman's injuries, but even
his indirect responsibility is enough for the law to hold him
liable, and enable the policeman to recover damages from
the car owner's insurance company. Surprising as it may
seem, the insurance company will be liable for the thief's
negligence in this situation not as a matter of general law,
but under special arrangements negotiated with the government (see below, p. 102).

There is another kind of defence – very similar to the defence of contributory negligence – which can sometimes be set up in negligence actions, and that is the defence of assumption of risk. It was at one time common for the defendant to argue that the plaintiff had voluntarily chosen to accept the risk of injury. Anybody who chooses to indulge in some risky activity may be thought to have only himself to blame if he is injured. But this defence too has been much curtailed by the judges over the years, especially where an employee sues his employer for unreasonably exposing him to a risk. It is, for instance, often said that an employee who is required to work under dangerous conditions is not truly acting voluntarily – he is being compelled to take the risks, so if he is injured the employer should be liable. Then too it is often said that the plaintiff may not have been fully informed about the risks – this argument is often raised when plaintiffs sue surgeons and hospitals for operations which go wrong. Unless the plaintiff is fully informed of the risks entailed by the operation, this defence against him will fail. So hospitals have now become much more careful and strict about warning patients of all the risks that may be involved in some medical or surgical procedure, even though many patients would probably rather be left in blissful ignorance.

This defence is likely to be especially important if actions against the tobacco companies for smoking-induced cancers ever come to court. The tobacco companies will doubtless argue that the risks of smoking have been public knowledge for at least forty years, so that anybody who has smoked must be regarded as having accepted the risks. The answer to that which the victims' lawyers are likely to make will probably be that the risks were not acknowledged by the tobacco companies, or even that they suppressed information about the risks, and perhaps also that because tobacco is addictive, smokers who were once hooked did not truly choose to continue smoking but simply were unable to give it up. If it is then suggested that, at least when the victims first started to smoke, they must have voluntarily chosen to do so, the plaintiffs' lawyers are likely to respond that most smokers have acquired the habit while they are still minors, and therefore not fully responsible for what they were doing. It will be seen that there is plenty of room for stretching things here too.

STRETCHING THE RULES OF CAUSATION

A basic requirement of a successful claim for damages for negligence is that the defendant must have *caused* the plaintiff's injuries. It is not enough to show that the defendant was negligent if the plaintiff would have suffered the same injuries anyhow. For instance if a hospital negligently fails to diagnose a patient's illness correctly, and the patient dies, no damages will be recoverable for his death if it is shown that the patient would have died even if his illness *had* been correctly diagnosed. The negligence in such a case is causally irrelevant.

The rules of causation often lead to difficulty in the law because of the problem of tracing the effects of an action through a long sequence of consequences. Even if the defendant was negligent in the first instance, how far does his liability extend when unusual or even bizarre events flow from his initial act of negligence? Generally speaking, a defendant's liability continues for most of the consequences of his negligence, even through a long sequence of events, so long as they are in a broad sense, natural or foreseeable outcomes.

The "egg-shell skull" rule

In personal injury cases these normal rules of causation are greatly modified in the plaintiff's favour by what lawyers know as "the egg-shell skull" rule. This says that if the plaintiff suffers from some idiosyncratic or rare condition (such as an abnormally thin skull) then any act of negligence which has much more serious consequences than could have been expected in the normal course of events, will still be treated as having been caused by the defendant. For instance, in a case in 1962 where a workman was slightly injured by a negligent colleague (for whom his employer was responsible) when a drop of hot liquid was splashed on his lip, and the splash triggered off a precancerous condition from which the plaintiff ultimately died, his death was actionable against the employer. And in another case in 1968 a post office worker grazed his knee slightly on a ladder on which he had slipped because some oil had been carelessly spilled on it; he was given a tetanus injection as a precaution but unfortunately had a freak reaction to the injection with devastating results. Here the only negligence consisted in spilling a little oil, but the employers were held liable for very substantial damages for the unfortunate consequences. An even more extreme case, perhaps, was decided by the House of Lords[3] in 1995. Here the plaintiff, who had suffered for 20 years from ME, (now normally called chronic fatigue syndrome) but who claimed to have been recovering, was involved in a minor road collision with the defendant, which was the latter's fault. Nobody was injured in the collision, and the plaintiff was able to drive home after the accident, but some hours later claimed to have felt the onset of a renewed attack of ME. He was awarded damages of over £162,000 on the ground that he would never be able to work again as a result of the defendant's negligence. This award was ultimately upheld after an appeal to the House of Lords.

It is hardly necessary to stress that decisions like this whittle away the distinction between negligence and pure

---

[3] The reader may need warning that the "House of Lords" referred to in this book is the final court of appeal for England, staffed by senior judges, and is not the legislative House of Lords which is the second House of Parliament, in which all peers and peeresses are entitled to sit.

accident, for which of course damages cannot be recovered at all. On the one hand the defendant's negligence is just being used as a mere excuse to make him liable for such bizarre consequences – nobody would regard the defendant as *morally* responsible for the extraordinary results in these three cases. On the other hand, looking at matters from the plaintiff's point of view, what is the relevant distinction, morally speaking, between a plaintiff who is injured or killed in such a freak way and one who is injured or killed by pure accident for which no one is to blame, and for which damages cannot be recovered at all? In each of these last three cases it is quite possible that some other event altogether would have triggered off the consequences which occurred. The pre-cancerous condition could have turned cancerous without external injury at all – such conditions often do turn cancerous; the post office worker who suffered the freak reaction to the tetanus injection might have had a tetanus injection for another reason at another time, and nobody could have been blamed at all; and the sufferer from ME might have had a recurrence of his illness for any number of reasons – ME tends to be like that.

Causation and the "blame culture"

There are other important kinds of cases where the rules of causation have been stretched in modern times, and these are especially interesting, because they reveal how this "stretching" is often a result of the "blame culture" in which we live. Suppose a person gives negligent advice to another, and the other person relies on that advice and loses some money as a result. Who has "caused" the ultimate loss? In one sense, of course, it must be the person who has acted on the advice – after all you don't *have* to act on advice, and if you choose to do so, you are (it may be thought) the author of your own misfortune. But this viewpoint, though it might be acceptable in a highly

individualistic society, has not been found acceptable in
modern times in Britain. Too often, as a practical matter,
we *do* have to rely on the advice of others, because we lack
the expertise to act by ourselves. This is obvious enough
when, say, you act on the advice of your doctor who negligently and wrongly tells you that you must stop work for
a month so you lose a month's pay; or perhaps even when
you rely on the advice of your central heating engineer
who mistakenly tells you that your boiler needs replacing
and acting on that advice costs you £500. But how far does
this go? Nobody would suggest that if you act on the
advice of a racing tipster and put £500 on a horse which
loses, you should be able to claim damages from the tipster.
It would be said that you acted on your own responsibility, and were the cause of your own loss. But in between
these two types of case there is a grey area where it is more
difficult to say whether you should be able to claim damages.

  There has, for instance, recently been a huge public out-
cry over the "scandal" of pension plans which have been
"wrongly sold" – that is, where employees have been
advised to move out of an employer's company pension
scheme and set up their own pension plan with an insurance company. It has been complained that much of the
advice given has been negligent and that employees have
lost by moving to these private pension plans – they would
have been better advised to stay with their company plans.
Rather surprisingly perhaps the insurance industry has
largely accepted these complaints and has promised to
compensate those who have suffered loss; yet it might have
been thought that a person bears some responsibility for
making his own financial decisions of this kind. Of course,
where there has been actual fraud or misrepresentation by
an insurance company or salesman, there must be proper
redress, but many of the complaints about these pension
plans appear to be nothing more than allegations that the

salesman gave "bad advice", which, on financial matters, is after all a matter of judgment and opinion. Perhaps these plans have been "wrongly bought" as much as "wrongly sold".

It is now being suggested[4] that an even more extensive responsibility rests on insurance companies who sell private pension plans. When these plans mature, there is a large capital sum available which has to be converted into a pension or annuity. The insured person is entitled to "buy" this annuity from the same insurance company or to have the capital value transferred to another insurance company and buy the annuity from them. The suggestion is that it is the responsibility of the first insurance company to tell the insured person that other companies may have better annuity rates than they do, and that he may be better off transferring the capital value elsewhere to buy his annuity. It has even been suggested that if the first company fails to do this they may be legally liable for damages. If these suggestions are right it will surely be proof that the legal system has finally gone mad! One might as well argue that when you apply to a company for motor insurance they ought to be legally bound to inform you that other companies have lower premiums, and you should be entitled to sue them if they fail to tell you this; or perhaps when someone buys a television set the sales assistant should be legally obliged to tell him that he could buy the same set more cheaply at a rival store.

It is unlikely that the law will ever go to such absurd extremes because judges say that parties relying on someone else's advice must take "reasonable" steps to protect their own interests. But how far you think it is reasonable to rely on advice given to you by others depends ultimately on whether you think people should make their own decisions, and stand on their own feet, or whether you believe

---

[4] See *Sunday Telegraph*, Business Section, 8 December 1996.

in a more paternalist society in which less well informed and more vulnerable people are enitled to rely on others. So the more paternalist a society gets, the more the blame culture develops, the more the public and perhaps the law will be inclined to say that losses caused to you by your own actions are "really" the result of someone else's negligence. This is one way the law can be stretched without the judges even realising what they are doing. We return to the theme of the "blame culture" in Chapter 6.

Omissions

There are other respects in which the rules of causation have been stretched in recent decades. In particular, they have been stretched to encompass many cases of negligence by *omission*. Suppose the plaintiff has been injured by the actions of X, but Y could have prevented X from causing the injuries or damage. Plainly X will be liable in this case, but X may be uninsured and not worth suing. Y, on the other hand, may be insured or may be a wealthy corporation or some public body, quite capable of paying the damages. So the plaintiff will try to sue Y. He has the difficulty of showing that Y has *caused* his injuries, but this is now often surmounted. There is no problem over the fact that X is obviously the main party responsible; the law has no difficulty in treating *both* X and Y as having caused the injuries, where appropriate. And, as we have already seen, it matters not one whit that the main, indeed, the overwhelming responsibility, may be X's. If any part of the responsibility, no matter how small, can be placed on Y, he can be sued for the entire loss, leaving him to get what joy he can out of a possible claim over against X for a share of the damages that he has to pay.

In order to establish a case against Y in this sort of situation the plaintiff will have to show some reason that Y should have prevented X from causing the damage. This will usually be found in some degree of control which Y may have over X. For example, in one leading case in 1970 known as *Dorset Yacht Co. v. Home Office*[5] some Home Office officials allowed a party of Borstal boys (as they used to be known) to escape onto the plaintiff's yacht where they did considerable damage. Obviously the Home Office officials did not directly cause the damage themselves – that was done by the Borstal boys. But the officials were in charge of the boys, and had negligently allowed them to escape from their control, so the Home Office was held liable for the damage.

Similarly, a school may be liable for negligently failing to control its pupils if they cause injury to other pupils, or perhaps, even if they escape and cause injury in school hours to persons outside the school. It is on this ground that the recent claim for damages by the ex-pupil who complained of bullying was presumably made against the school authority.

In rare cases this kind of liability may even be imposed on someone who fails to prevent a person from deliberately injuring *himself*. In 1970 there was a rather remarkable case of a hospital being held liable to a known psychiatric and suicidal risk who injured himself when he jumped out of the window. This is the kind of case which can make the law look absurd when taken out of context, but it is perfectly in accordance with modern legal principles. More commonly, this kind of liability would be imposed on a defendant for injury to children under his control – for instance a schoolteacher could be liable for allowing a young child to injure itself.

Another modern instance of the stretching of the rules of causation in cases of omissions is the statutory liability of highway authorities for damage or injury caused by their *failure to repair* the highway. Until 1961 highway authorities were only liable for damage or injury caused by badly executed repairs, but now their liability extends to cases of non-repair as well. At first sight this seems a relatively minor change, but actually it is really quite a major one. Obviously if repairs are actually carried out, it will not normally be more costly to do them properly than to do them negligently, so the burden on the highway authority to see that they are done properly is not unduly severe. But the liability for non-repair actually imposes a duty on highway authorities regularly to inspect their roads (and pavements, which are legally part of the highway) and then to repair them should defects or dangers appear. In fact every local authority (which is the highway authority for urban roads) is now constantly having to meet claims for damages by members of the public who claim they have injured themselves by tripping over protruding paving stones and the like. It is, of course, very difficult to verify these claims, and no doubt rather easy to exaggerate their seriousness. Yet the cost of meeting them, or trying to avoid them by constantly repairing the roads and pavings, has to compete with other demands on local authority spending, such as schools, police expenditure and so on. Fortunately a recent decision of the House of Lords has put a stop to some of the more extreme possibilities, such as holding a local authority liable for failing to actually *improve* its roads, rather than just to maintain them in repair. This case is further discussed in Chapter 3 (see p. 83).

STRETCHING THE KINDS OF INJURY YOU CAN CLAIM DAMAGES FOR

At one time damages for injury, especially for personal injury, were almost entirely confined to cases where the victim suffered a plain and obvious physical injury. These are the obvious and straightforward results of many physical acts of negligence – road accidents, damages in factories, and the like.

But in recent years the law here too has been stretched in half a dozen different directions. First, it has come to be recognised – indeed it has never really been doubted – that damages can be recovered for any physical harm, not just for ordinary injuries. So for example, if a person contracts even an ordinary illness as a result of somebody's negligence, that is now plainly actionable. So if a person is unreasonably exposed to the risk of contagion in a hospital, for instance, and catches even a perfectly ordinary disease – bronchitis, say – he can get damages for that. (Of course, most victims of bronchitis can't recover damages for it because they can't prove it was the result of anybody else's negligence.) Similarly, anybody who suffers from a disease as a result of being exposed to some unreasonable risk at their place of employment, can recover damages if he can prove the necessary facts. Many miners and asbestos workers who have contracted lung diseases or cancers in recent years have recovered damages. Some have, unfortunately, died, and then their families may have been able to claim compensation. The family of someone who dies prematurely from other cancers or illnesses, not contracted in this way, have no such claims even though, from their point of view, the result is exactly the same.

Then there are claims by or on behalf of babies injured in the course of or the aftermath of birth. It is tragically true that many babies suffer terrible brain damage as a result of birth injuries, and injuries like this are actually more common today than they were formerly – until recently the babies would have died because of the then state of medical science. Today frantic efforts are often made by doctors and hospitals to save the lives of these babies but sometimes, unfortunately, at the price of brain damage or other severe side effects like blindness. Provided negligence can be proved, heavy damages can be recovered for these injuries or conditions, against the very doctors and hospitals responsible for saving the baby's life.

There is another type of case where damages have been awarded for the unexpected physical consequences of medical procedures, even where they cannot be said to be injuries at all. Damages have occasionally been awarded against hospitals for badly performed sterilisation procedures, with the result that a child has been born. Giving birth is hardly a physical injury, but it does cost quite a lot to maintain a child for the whole 18 years of its minority, and if lawyers so arrange matters that this cost can be passed onto a negligent surgeon, or a Trust Hospital or Health Authority, no doubt some people will take advantage of the law. Some, indeed, have. (Scots judges have declined to follow this particular piece of English folly.)

Second, purely cosmetic injury – something which affects your appearance rather than your physical well-being – is also plainly actionable. The case of the boy who claimed for the discolouration of his teeth is a simple example. And despite sex equality laws, nearly all judges will award more damages to a girl or young woman than to a man, for a cosmetic injury – a small scar on her face or even on her body which would prevent her wearing a bikini, for instance.

Attempts to push the boundaries of the law even further were recently made, but have so far been rebuffed by the courts. In 1995 several actions by children and their families were brought against local authorities for failing to take reasonable care in the exercise of their statutory powers to protect the children from potential abuse, or, conversely, to separate the children from their parents in cases of suspected abuse when in fact there was none, and in yet other cases, for failing to make special educational provision for children with special learning needs. In some of these cases the children suffered physical harm but in others the kind of harm being complained about did not really fall within any of the traditional areas of the law – the mental distress caused to a child and parent by their being forcibly separated, or to a child not being offered appropriate educational provision is really of a wholly new kind despite attempts by their lawyers to claim that they were suffering from "anxiety neurosis". All these claims failed on highly complex legal grounds, more to do with the undesirability of imposing legal liabilities of this kind on local authorities, but doubtless also influenced by the fact that the kind of harm complained about here was wholly outside the law's traditional areas of concern.

Another decision, also in 1995, rejected claims for damages against the Crown Prosecution Service by two accused persons who were detained pending trial, but released when the prosecutions were abandoned. In both cases the essential complaint was that the Crown Prosecution Service had been negligent in not appreciating at an early enough stage that the evidence was too weak too justify the prosecutions. Of course the "injury" being complained of here was that the men were in jail pending trial, and that kind of injury has always been remediable by a special action for malicious prosecution which requires proof of "malice" or improper motive; but this was the first time that someone had tried to obtain damages merely on the ground of negligence in such a case.

The attempt to dream up new kinds of harm for which damages may be recovered goes on all the time. Even as this book was written a solicitor announced that legal aid had been granted to enable him to pursue a claim for damages on behalf of two schoolchildren against their schools (presumably local education authority schools) for failing to give them a decent education, so that they failed to pass their GCSE examinations and had to spend another year at school to retake them.[6] It is very unlikely that these claims can succeed, and it seems astonishing that legal aid should have been granted for them to proceed at all, in view of the

[6] *The Times*, 2 December 1996, p. 4.

decision of the House of Lords against similar claims only last year. But of course if claims like this do succeed schools will probably have to take out (or spend more on) insurance against the risk of being sued on this ground, and money which could be spent on improving the educational facilities will be diverted to paying insurance companies (and lawyers).

Mental injury

By far the most worrying development in the law relating to the kind of harm for which you can recover damages, however, has been the huge growth of claims in recent years for damages for "nervous or emotional shock" or, what nowadays tends to be called post-traumatic stress. The law on this point is quite complicated, and still not settled by the courts in various particulars. Only a bare summary will be offered here. It must first be understood that the courts have always refused to award damages for bare mental distress or grief, *except to those who also suffer physical injury*. Obviously when people are seriously injured or killed in accidents, close relatives of the primary victims will often be severely shocked and grief-stricken. But this has never been allowed to develop of its own into actionable injury. Of course if damages were awarded for mere grief or shock, then parents and close relatives of every child injured or killed in an accident would be able to recover damages on their own behalf, but the law does not go that far as a general rule. The death of a young child allows the parents to recover only a fixed sum, now £7,500, as damages for bereavement, which is technically payable to the child's estate, regardless of the parents' grief or shock.

But what has happened in the past few years is that the courts have increasingly come to recognise that many close relatives of primary accident victims may suffer more severe consequences than grief or distress, however prolonged. Sometimes, the mental reactions may be very severe – leading to deep depressions, or even suicidal tendencies. Often there are (or are claimed to be) a variety of other symptoms present, such as inability to work, sleeplessness, nightmares, and so on. The judges have been torn by their desire to award damages in the most serious of these cases, while not opening the floodgates to every single relative or parent of primary accident victims. So they have allowed some of these claimants to obtain damages, but to keep the numbers within limits they have insisted on two conditions: (1) the claimant must have suffered a *recognisable psychiatric illness or condition*, and not just be suffering from grief or deep unhappiness, however prolonged and serious in itself; and (2) the claimant must have witnessed the accident, or been sufficiently close to it, in time and space to make his reaction a foreseeable one, and not something quite extraordinary. This means that close relatives of primary victims who actually witness a particularly horrifying accident or disaster, and are close to the scene when it occurs, or even come upon its aftermath almost immediately, may be able to recover damages for psychological illness consequent on what they have seen. Others more remote from the immediate scene, or less closely connected with the primary victims are unlikely to be able to claim, although in specially strong circumstances mere bystanders may be able to recover. In the legal actions following the Hillsborough football stadium disaster in 1989 many claims were made for damages for shock and psychiatric illness by relatives of those injured and killed. In general, those who only saw the events on television were not permitted to recover, and even among those in the stadium itself, damages were not awarded except to the closest relatives such as parents or (in one case) a fiancé.

But the tendency to "stretch" the law goes on all the time, especially, perhaps, when settlements are being negotiated. In November 1996, for instance, the Lincolnshire

Health Authority paid half a million pounds to settle claims for post-traumatic stress by the parents of thirteen children bizarrely killed or injured by their nurse Beverly Allitt who was convicted of manslaughter.[7] These parents were not at the immediate scene of the hospital when the deaths or injuries occurred, though naturally they visited their children while they were still alive in the hospital. Moreover, damages in these cases are only supposed to be awarded to plaintiffs who suffer genuine psychiatric disorders, and it is hard to credit that *all* these parents were suffering from such disorders, as opposed to merely natural human grief for the deaths or injuries to their children. It must be understood that the injured children, and the estates (that is, the parents) of the children who had been killed, had already received damages from the Health Authority for the injuries and deaths. The half million pound settlement was for the parents for their *own* trauma. In the fatal cases the parents recovered twice over, since money received by the estate of a small child is necessarily passed on to the parents (a young child cannot make a will, so its heirs will always be its parents.)

Yet another claim in 1996 was allowed by a judge, though later overturned by the Court of Appeal.[8] In this case a Health Authority discovered that an obstetrics worker in the hospital was infected with HIV, and though the risk of infection for patients was extremely low, it wrote to 900 patients who had been in contact with the worker, advising them of what they had discovered, and offering them HIV testing, counselling and advice. Not one of these patients actually proved to be HIV positive, but 114 of them sued the hospital for anxiety and shock. It was not suggested that the hospital had been in any way negligent in employing the obstetrics worker or in failing to discover that she was HIV positive; but it was claimed

[7] *The Times*, 28 November 1996.
[8] *The Times*, 27 November 1996.

that the hospital had been negligent in sending out letters, rather than in calling in the patients for personal face to face consultations at which counselling could have been immediately available. The trial judge agreed, though once again it is almost beyond belief that 114 patients out of 900 should have suffered from recognised psychiatric illnesses (as distinguished from natural worry or anxiety) through the receipt of the warning letter. As already indicated, the Appeal Court threw out the case.

Other claims stemming from the Hillsborough stadium disaster made by a number of policemen on duty at the stadium have recently been permitted by the Court of Appeal (though they may yet be carried to the House of Lords on further appeal), on the ground that policemen attempting to render assistance in a disaster fall within the category of "rescuers", a group long favoured by the law, who are often allowed to sue when others cannot. In particular, rescuers cannot normally be defeated by the argument that they have themselves been guilty of contributory negligence or that they voluntarily assumed the risk of injury. The Court of Appeal's decision in these cases has been greeted with considerable indignation by many members of the public, some of whom have written letters to the newspapers pointing out that policemen, members of the emergency services and the armed forces and others similarly placed, have always been expected to encounter traumatic and horrifying events in the course of their duties, and it is difficult to see why they should be better treated than the relatives of many of the killed and injured who watched the tragedy on television. To be fair, many members of emergency services and armed forces have also written letters to the press taking the same line, pointing out that literally millions of them suffered traumatic and horrifying experiences in the last war, and insisting that they would never contemplate suing in such circumstances.

There is considerable force in these criticisms of the court's decision, which if left standing, may have profound significance far beyond the case in hand. Is a hospital now bound to ensure that its nurses and emergency staff (serving perhaps in casualty units) are adequately sheltered from, or able to cope with the effects, of what they see in their daily work? Is every police force bound to take care that its young and untried staff can cope with murder and mayhem and other emergencies which they may encounter? And what about members of the armed services? Of course, as always, negligence must be proved before damages can be recovered, but it is easy to see how a plaintiff can argue that the mere failure to give adequate training beforehand, or counselling afterwards, itself amounts to negligence in certain circumstances. Many people work in stressful employment of one kind or another (though some of the unemployed might think they are lucky to be in work at all) and recent years have seen increasing numbers of claims for damages for stress and anxiety against employers, in some of which very substantial damages have been awarded. One might think that if a person cannot cope with the stress of his job he simply ought to find a less stressful job. President Truman was once credited with the advice, "If you can't stand the heat, get out of the kitchen". Now, it would seem more accurate to say, "If you can't stand the heat go and see a solicitor."

One reason why these claims cause particular difficulty is that the legal requirement that the plaintiff must prove he has suffered from a recognisable psychiatric condition does not seem to have worked very well as a way of identifying really genuine cases. It must be said that the medical profession – like the judges themselves – are very sympathetic to those who claim to have suffered such psychiatric conditions. A patient whose close relative has been involved in a serious accident, or who has witnessed a serious accident affecting, perhaps, a young child, may well suffer great mental distress and shock. But it is not really obvious that doctors are much better than judges at separating those who merely suffer from normal grief and shock, from those who actually suffer from some real illness. So many of the symptoms of these psychiatric conditions appear to be subjective – depressions, loss of interest in life, inability to work or to sleep well, etc., etc., – that one is entitled to feel sceptical over the prevalence of these conditions among those who claim damages. Giving these perfectly natural conditions fancy names like "post-traumatic stress" does not actually demonstrate that they have a real, objective existence, though judges striving not to appear old-fashioned fuddy duddies, are naturally persuaded by the doctors that they have.

One particularly worrying feature of these cases is that predictions about the plaintiff's long-term employment prospects are (or appear to be) especially suspect. When a person has an objectively serious physical condition it is easy to predict that he may be unable to work again; but when the condition is entirely mental, such predictions seem more dubious – and indeed, as events have shown, sometimes prove quite unreliable (for one such case see p. 11 above). Yet enormous damages awards are sometimes based on these predictions.

It is interesting to note that the social security system has been suffering from exactly the same problems as the law of tort. Until 1994 anybody who suffered from long-term disability was entitled to social security invalidity benefit, but claims for long-term invalidity had soared from 600,000 in 1978-79 to almost 1.5 million in 1992-93 at a time when the nation's health was generally improving. All these claims were, of course, backed by doctors who readily enough certified that their patients were incapable of work. Since the health of the nation was generally improving over this fifteen year period, it seems likely that much of the increase in claims for invalidity benefit stemmed from depressive and other psychological or mental conditions. In 1994 the government responded to this massive (and costly) growth by abolishing invalidity benefit and replacing it with incapacity benefit – and the claimants for incapacity benefit are required to prove rather more objective symptoms of their inability to work. Perhaps the judges should follow suit.

There is one other reason why claims by policemen and other emergency workers for damages for psychiatric injury are particularly undeserving. Most employees in these categories work under statutory schemes which permit them to retire on pension if they suffer injuries or disabling conditions arising out of their employment. So a policeman who is so traumatized by something he encounters in his work that he is compelled to give up his work is already substantially better off than many other members of the public in a similar situation. Of course this does not prevent their seeking damages as well if they are legally entitled to them (in which case they are still entitled to their pensions, and no deductions are made from the damages on account of them), but it is a reason for thinking that sympathy for the claimants of damages may sometimes be misplaced.

Economic loss

There is one other kind of damage which a plaintiff may sometimes wish to claim for, and which can give rise to very difficult questions of law and policy, and that is, a claim for *pure* economic or pecuniary loss, without any physical (or even mental) injury. Suppose a contractor negligently cuts through a power cable while he is digging up the road to repair a drain or telephone cable. The result may be to deprive local consumers, and even local businesses and factories, of their power supply for a few hours or perhaps longer. This may cause not just inconvenience, but actual financial loss, for instance, to a company whose factory has to close for half a day. Claims of this kind were unknown to the law until modern times, and even today they are not generally allowed at all. The main reason for this is the purely pragmatic consideration that if such claims were once allowed the possible consequences could be limitless. All sorts of people may suffer financial loss when some physical injury or damage is caused to another person or his property. In the case of the power cable, for instance, the factory owner may not be the only person to suffer financial loss – perhaps his workers may also suffer losses of earnings (for overtime, for example), and his customers may also suffer financial loss through delayed deliveries. What is more, each of these parties may be connected with further persons who in turn suffer money losses when they suffer. If the factory owner's workers suffer lost wages, perhaps the local pub owner also suffers, and the local football team may find its takings down that week, and so on. Plainly, the repercussions of losses like this are endless, and it is perfectly sensible of the courts to refuse to allow actions to be brought in such circumstances.

However, things do not stop there. If the claim is for pure economic loss, you can't generally sue for damages in an ordinary negligence action (as we have just seen) but you can sue for *breach of contract*, and there are some actions for breach of contract which are very similar to negligence actions. We have already discussed a number of cases concerning pension plans sold by insurance companies, where even claims for purely economic loss are being met, because there was a contractual liability for negligence (see p. 48). But allowing claims of this kind for breach of contract brings with it a very worrying possibility, namely that some contractual claims for damages for negligence can be for such fantastic sums of money that the legal system simply cannot cope properly with the consequences, and even if it could, the resulting social and commercial dislocation would be in nobody's real interest. In particular the potential liability of firms of accountants, where they have been involved in professional auditing or giving advice in multi-million pound business activities, is simply astronomical. Suppose one company wishes to take over another at a cost of several billion pounds – by no means an abnormal business deal these days. Before making its take-over offer the buying company (call them A) will wish to satisfy themselves of the value of the second company (let's call them B). For this purpose they will have to rely on accountants who will examine what books and documents they can, and may then give A the necessary assurances. If the accountants have been negligent it may turn out eventually that B is worth much less than A anticipated, and A may feel aggrieved – indeed, they may feel so aggrieved that they may try to claim damages against the accountants for negligence. If this were purely a negligence claim it would not be permitted, but because the accountants will have been working for A under a contract for their professional services, an action for negligence is in principle available. Indeed, it is not really problematical in law. The only real problem is that, according to ordinary legal principles, the accountants may be liable for damages running into hundreds of millions of pounds, or occasionally even more.

There is absolutely nothing fanciful about this scenario. Many of the world's leading accountancy firms (which are enormous organizations) are currently being threatened with law suits whose total value certainly does run into hundreds of millions of pounds. Firms of solicitors may also find themselves threatened by similar liabilities. It is no answer to this problem to say that accountants and solicitors should insure against their liabilities – they already do, but even insurance companies are unwilling to cover liabilities of this sort of magnitude. Most firms will find it impossible to obtain insurance cover for liabilities much in excess of £50 million, so if firms actually are rendered liable for such damages, each of the partners will be liable to his last penny. Partners in professional firms (like accountants, solicitors, doctors and so forth) do not operate like businessmen under the protection of the limited liability system. In business, companies may go bankrupt, and shareholders will then lose what they have invested in them, but the directors of the company are not as a matter of general law personally liable for the company's debts. But partners are so liable, and a massive liability which exceeds the firm's insurance cover could leave them bankrupted, their houses and other assets seized to pay the debt, and the firm itself completely broken up and liquidated. All this could follow from a single act of negligence, a single piece of negligent advice.

These potential consequences are just absurd, and totally disproportionate to the gravity of the fault which may have led to the liability. They are also completely contrary to the public interest since large firms of accountants are socially and commercially useful bodies of well qualified professional people, whose services are in constant need. The result of these fears is that many large firms of accountants are today seeking ways of limiting the personal liability of their partners, for example, by operating as limited liability companies, or setting up their head office abroad in some country whose laws might protect them. There are serious difficulties about either of these courses, however, and for the moment, the threat to large professional firms from this kind of litigation remains a very real one.

What this tends to show is that it is only the existence of insurance which makes most of the law of negligence acceptable, and where insurance is unavailable, the law is not acceptable nor fair nor in the public interest. Fortunately, in the case of ordinary injury and accident claims, where physical damage and injury is in question, the liabilities are so much lower than these potential astronomical financial losses, that insurance is readily available. We return to this important question in Chapter 5.

3. MORE STRETCHING OF THE LAW

STRETCHING THE DAMAGES WHICH CAN BE AWARDED

A SIMPLE outline of the principles on which damages are assessed has already been given. Here it is proposed to add a few words to show how modern changes in the law nearly always seem to favour the plaintiff, and enhance the damages available. These changes have by no means come purely from the judges. Many of them have come from Parliament, and many of them have also followed recommendations from the Law Commission. All this goes to show how powerful is the pressure constantly to improve the position of those who claim damages for injury and death. In Chapter 6 we shall see in some detail why this policy is so mistaken, even though it largely stems from a natural sympathy and compassion for the injured. Here, the reader is asked to keep in the forefront of his mind that for every accident victim who obtains damages, there may be eight or nine other victims of similar accidents, and probably a further ninety disabled persons whose incapacity does not derive from an accident, who obtain none.

The rules relating to the assessment of damages for injuries have not changed greatly in the past thirty or forty years, and it is actually difficult to say how far, allowing for inflation, damage awards have increased. Damages for pecuniary losses, as we have seen, include principally earnings losses and medical costs of various kinds. Since real earnings have obviously gone up a good deal in recent decades and medical costs have also increased far higher than the general rate of inflation, it is entirely natural to expect that the total sums awarded for pecuniary losses should also have gone up a good deal. Damages for non-pecuniary losses may, as we have previously seen, have actually gone down slightly, though this is probably more than offset by the fact that so many new and different types of loss are nowadays included as separate items in the damages for pecuniary losses.

It does seem certain at least that *maximum* awards of damages (including both pecuniary and non-pecuniary elements) in the most serious cases of all have increased very dramatically in the past thirty years. In 1968 the Court of Appeal reduced a then unprecedentedly high award of some £66,000 to about £51,000 in a case of high earnings and maximum severity. So this can be taken as the benchmark for the highest sort of award then thought permissible. But today maximum awards in the worst cases exceed two or three million pounds in value (some of these are today made as part of a "structured settlement" in which the money is actually paid over in the form of an annuity, rather than a lump sum). Maximum awards therefore appear to have increased by about thirty to fifty times during these thirty years, while earnings in general have increased by ten or twelve times during the same period.

Other changes which have improved the position of plaintiffs with regard to the size of damages include the statutory requirement, introduced in 1969, that damages awarded for personal injuries should now include interest unless there are special reasons to the contrary. Given the long delays often involved in the settlement or trial of these cases, the entitlement to interest often raises the total damages by as much as ten or even twenty percent.

Another change – as a result of judicial decisions – has been to give additional damages to an accident victim who has been nursed or cared for by a relative. Judges thought it unfair that if the plaintiff was so badly injured that he needed to employ someone to care for him, and paid wages to that person, the wages would be a recoverable item of damages, while if his wife or parent (for instance) took on the burden for love rather than money, nothing should be paid. So the plaintiff is now entitled to recover an additional sum for these care costs, even though they are not actually incurred.

In a case in 1994 a young motor cyclist seriously injured his pillion passenger who he later married. Commendably, he took care of her at home in her injured state. In an action nominally against her husband, she recovered over £600,000 in damages, which included a sum of £77,000 which was intended as a recompense for her husband's care of her. This sum was struck out on appeal because the House of Lords decided that, as the husband was himself the wrongdoer, he could not expect to be paid for providing the care which his own negligence had made necessary. The Law Commission has recently proposed that this decision be reversed so that in such cases the carer should be recompensed for his work. This recommendation makes no sense except on the assumption that the legal "wrong" on which the liability is based is a technical, minor matter of no importance, and that in reality the right to compensation is based on insurance and not on wrongdoing. But once that conclusion is reached, the *whole system* makes no sense – why should a person suffering similar injuries to this young woman be unable to obtain any damages at all (let alone the extra £77,000) if the accident was not due to someone's fault?

Another judge-made rule has gone through several fluctuations in recent years. This rule concerns the question of offsetting benefits. When a plaintiff is injured he is often entitled to other benefits from other sources, quite apart from any damages. Should the damages be reduced to take account of these benefits? Suppose, for instance, the plaintiff is a police officer who has to retire, with a police pension, as a result of being injured in an accident. Should the damages be reduced because of the pension? No, said the House of Lords in 1969, and the police officer in that case ended up, not only with damages and a police pension but also with a social security pension as well. In later cases attempts have been made to persuade the courts to award damages for losses of earning even though the earnings were in fact made up by the employer, but these attempts have failed. The line must be drawn somewhere, even when all allowance is made for sympathy for the plaintiff. If he has not lost any earnings he cannot recover damages for lost earnings.

Similar problems arise with regard to social security benefits payable to accident victims. In this respect the plaintiff's position has actually been made worse in recent years – one of the very few modern legal changes which operate to the disadvantage of plaintiffs in personal injury actions. At one time any social security benefits the plaintiff might have been paid were largely ignored in the assessment of the damages – a small deduction was made for some (but not all) of the benefits. More recently the government has made serious efforts to claw back larger sums of benefit from the damages under a complex set of statutory provisions. These are too technical to discuss in detail, but they only apply to damage awards exceeding £2,500. Below this sum, the plaintiff is entitled to keep his damages and his benefits, subject only to the minor deduction arrangements previously in force, as mentioned above. Above the £2,500 figure, the insurer paying the damages must deduct the full value of any social security benefits paid in respect of the injury and pay the money over to the DSS. Of course these are not designed to reduce the plaintiff's total compensation, but only to cut down on the duplication involved where the plaintiff obtains benefits while his legal claim is proceeding, and then perhaps recovers a large sum which is entirely adequate to repay the benefits, and, often, still leave him plenty left over.

In fatal cases the law is particularly favourable to the claims of dependants, and especially widows (and less commonly, widowers). In these cases, there is virtually no attempt to avoid duplication at all, and many a widow must have been relieved to discover that her financial position after her husband has been killed in an accident has actually improved, sometimes quite substantially. For instance, all life insurance benefits are, by express statutory provision, excluded from the calculation of the damages, and so are pension entitlements under the deceased's employment scheme, and social security pension entitlements. Furthermore, by another express statutory provision passed in 1971 (on a free parliamentary vote) the fact or possibility of a widow's remarriage is also excluded from consideration. Since many young widows do remarry, often within a year or two, and since it often takes some time for their cases to reach court or to be settled, it is by no means unknown for damages to be awarded to a widow for the loss she suffered on the death of her (first) husband, while she is happily married to a wealthier husband. In America it is not unknown for a widow to be married to husband no. 3 before her claim to damages for the loss of husband no. 1 is disposed of. If the case goes to court, the fact of the remarriages then has to be concealed from the jury who are sometimes faced with a widow dressed in black, and carrying the prescribed handkerchief, with which she wipes her eyes delicately from time to time. We avoid this farce in England – but the damages still have to be assessed as though she had not remarried.

In one extreme case a wealthy man had made substantial donations amounting to some £40,000 to a child, and had then taken out life insurance to cover the risk of early death with a consequent liability for £17,000 additional death duties. When he was killed in an accident his family obtained the benefits of the life insurance, and were able to recover, as an additional item of damages, the £17,000 from the defendant. In other words they obtained the £17,000 twice over, from different sources. Some people may be inclined to say: well, good luck to a plaintiff who recovers these windfall sums. But before taking this view, it is necessary to remember that the cost of all these damages is ultimately falling on the public, as we shall see in more detail later.

The cost of assessing the damages

The damages awarded for the injuries the plaintiff has suffered, and the probable future effect of these damages on his employment prospects and indeed, his whole life style, are, in many serious cases, matters of considerable difficulty and trouble to assess. Many medical and consultants' reports may be needed for this purpose, often involving several different consultants (usually one for the plaintiff and another for the defendant), and often being repeated over a period of time before the claim is finalised. And of course while consultants are seeing patients for this purpose they are the less available for NHS duties. In addition, the plaintiff's more social needs – adapting a house, installing special facilities to enable a disabled plaintiff to cope with a kitchen or bathroom, and so on – may nowadays be assessed by other experts. This is, of course, a Rolls Royce service. All these consultants and experts will be privately engaged and paid substantial professional fees and expenses. These costs will ultimately have to be paid for by the defendant (or his insurers) if the action succeeds. If the plaintiff is on legal aid, they will be paid by the legal aid authorities if the action fails. The care and attention lavished on plaintiffs in this situation can be contrasted with the sort of frugal fare meted out to ordinary social services clients.

STRETCHING THE NUMBER
OF PEOPLE YOU CAN SUE

Spouses

Do you know that you can sue your husband or wife for damages? Well, you may say, (unless you happen to be considering divorce) what's the point? The point, of course, is that your spouse won't actually have to pay – an insurance company will pay. If one spouse injures the other through negligence, the ordinary rules of law now apply. This happens commonly enough when one spouse is driving a car and the other spouse is a passenger in the car. Until 1962 spouses could not sue each other for torts, and until 1971 passengers often could not obtain damages for injuries in car accidents because insurance policies did not have to cover them. The law on both points having now been altered by Parliament in favour of injured parties, the result is that a spouse can now claim in this kind of case.

Of course negligence must, as always, be proved. But a spouse who has injured another spouse while driving has only to admit that he was going too fast, or failing to keep an adequate look-out, or overtaking dangerously, and the trick is done. The insurance company may try to argue that he was driving with all due care, but if he gives evidence in court, they are going to have a hard job defending the action when it is so obviously in his interest to lose it. The two spouses can, as the saying goes, laugh all the way to the bank – or perhaps take a good holiday on the proceeds. Of course there are also tragic cases where the injuries are too serious to be a cause for rejoicing, no matter how generous the compensation.

The same thing can happen with accidents in the home, but before trying it on, check your insurance policy. It is not compulsory for home insurance policies (as opposed to motor policies) to cover liability to other members of the family, and some do not do so. Bear in mind also, that even in the case of motor accidents, a spouse can only obtain damages from the insurance company if the other spouse was negligent in *the course of driving or using the car.* If your spouse nags you to distraction while you are driving, and an accident results in which you are injured, you can't get at the insurance company because they are only answerable for negligent driving, not for nagging spouses. But the passenger-spouse may be able to get at the insurance company, because a reasonably careful driver should not allow himself (or herself) to be distracted by a nagging spouse. It is also necessary to remember that you cannot sue yourself. If you are entirely responsible for your own injuries there is no way you can get damages for the result, though (as we have seen, p. 43) with a bit of ingenuity your lawyer may be able to show that you were not solely to blame, and that somebody else was partly to blame.

Everybody understands perfectly well what is going on in these inter-family cases. Introducing the law of negligence is purely a device to help the parties get compensation from an insurance company – it is not intended to be taken seriously. But, of course, in the end the law's requirements do have to be satisfied if damages are to be obtained in this way so a family can obtain damages if one spouse injures the other, but not if one spouse injures himself, or herself. There is no sense in this.

Suing the estate of a deceased wrongdoer

At one time you could not sue the estate of a deceased wrongdoer at all. The idea was that a tort was a personal wrong, and if the person who committed it had died there was no point in allowing an action. But then road accidents became common, and in a bad road accident the person to blame may himself be killed in the accident. What was more, insurance became compulsory for road accidents, so there seemed no reason why the insurance company should not pay even if the wrongdoer was dead. So the law was changed in 1934 and actions of this kind came to be permitted.

That may have been a perfectly reasonable reform, but it also applies to family cases, which may sometimes produces some pretty odd results. For instance if a husband injures his wife in an accident in which he is killed, she can still claim against his estate (and therefore his insurance company) which is perhaps understandable; but if they are *both* killed in the accident, their dependent children can sue the estate of the parent who was driving and get damages for being deprived of their other parent. So if both parents of a young child die from natural causes, there will be no compensation, but if one kills the other by negligence, damages can be obtained. Again, there seems no sense in these distinctions.

The liability of employers

There is a very important set of rules in the law known as the doctrine of vicarious liability. Under this doctrine an employer is legally answerable for the negligence of an employee committed in the course of his employment. It is not necessary to show that the employer was himself or itself in any way to blame or negligent for what has happened. Employers may, of course, be careless in their selection of employees, or in failing to supervise them adequately, or in failing to check their qualifications, and so on. Even these forms of negligence may well be the negligence of other employees, more senior ones, such as managers and so on, but it is possible for companies to be negligent on their own account, as it were, and not just as a result of what their employees have done, so companies may be liable either for their own negligence, or vicariously liable for the negligence of their employees. But when the plaintiff claims against an employer under the doctrine of vicarious liability he does not have to show that the company was itself negligent at all. All that he has to show is that the person who was negligent was an employee, and that he was working on the job when the negligence occurred.

This means that a huge number of accidents and injuries can and do lead to claims against employers. Every bus driver, every lorry driver, every factory worker, may make his employer liable if he negligently injures any person in the course of his employment. This doctrine is by no means new – it has been with us at least since 1700; and even its great expansion was mostly achieved in the last century. One very important change was, however, introduced in 1948. Until then, one employee could not generally sue the employer for the negligence of another employee if they were in "common employment", that is, working together. This meant that the doctrine of vicarious liability was most important, generally speaking, in creating legal liability to the public – to those outside the employment or business in question. But since 1948, employers have been liable to one employee who is injured by the negligence of another employee, and this kind of liability has vastly increased in scope and importance over the years. A good proportion of all work accidents (at least ten percent and possibly many more) today lead to claims for damages against the employer.

Apart from this one major change in the doctrine of vicarious liability, what has happened in this century has been little more than minor tidying up – though once again always in favour of plaintiffs. For example, one way in which the doctrine has been extended in the past forty or fifty years concerns the definition of an employee. At one time professional people like doctors were thought to be excluded from the doctrine, but that idea has long since disappeared. Doctors employed by hospitals are now treated like any other employee. GPs, it is true, are not employed by the Health Service, but are self-employed, but anyhow that does not matter for our purposes, because even if they have no employer, they have insurers.

The second way in which the doctrine has been expanded in modern times is by stretching the concept of the employee's "course of employment", that is, by treating the worker as engaged on his job even when he was doing something he clearly should not have been doing. The doctrine is easiest to understand, and perhaps to justify, where the employee is actually engaged in doing the very thing he is employed to do when the negligence occurs, but today the doctrine is very much wider than this. An employer may be liable, for instance, even where the employee has been doing something entirely for his own purposes and benefit, while still generally doing his work. So an employee at a filling station who smoked while on duty, and caused a fire, rendered his employer liable. And the employer may be liable even where the employee does an act which is expressly forbidden, so long as the employee is still engaged in the general class of acts he is employed to do. An employee who is, for instance, required to clean some electrical machinery in a factory, but is expressly forbidden from doing so unless the machine is first switched off, may still render his employer liable if he cleans the machinery without switching it off. The nurse Beverly Allitt who killed and injured several patients by deliberately giving them the wrong drugs, or excessive doses, was clearly acting in the course of her employment as a nurse in the legal sense, and so the hospital had to accept liability for her actions. (If she had tried to perform an operation on a patient, that would, however, have plainly been outside the course of her employment altogether.) Similarly, prison warders who place a prisoner in a "strip cell" and forcibly strip him contrary to Prison Regulations may render the Home Office liable for their actions, so long as they amount only to a "misguided and unauthorised method of performing their duties" rather than acts right outside the scope of their normal duties. It is only where the employee is off "on a frolic of his own" as a famous judgment once expressed it, that the employer will not be liable.

Vicarious liability also applies to partners, who are liable for each other's actions in the course of working for the partnership. This is one of the things that causes such trouble with professional firms as we saw earlier (p. 64). Very large firms of accountants may have several hundred partners, and each partner has to accept full legal responsibility for the liabilities of his colleagues in the course of their work. The partners are all liable for their employees as well, under the ordinary rules of vicarious liability.

The law of vicarious liability does not exonerate the employee guilty of negligence from liability – all that it does is to make the employer liable as well as the employee. Since the plaintiff is entitled to sue any of the parties who is legally responsible to him, he can sue the employer alone, and recover in full from him even though the employer is entirely free of any moral responsibility and the whole blame rests on the employee. In legal theory the employer, having paid the damages, could claim reimbursement from the employee. But in practice this never happens. Employers do not want to antagonise their workforces by making such claims, and in the social and employment context the legal culture which treats negligence as a blameworthy fault is entirely absent. Most people assume that ordinary acts of everyday negligence (such the careless driving of a lorry) are not seriously blameworthy acts, and that it would be unfair to penalise their employees for committing such acts, for which anyhow, the employer is usually insured. Where the fault is more serious the employee may be disciplined, or even dismissed for his acts, but it is almost unheard of for the employer to claim that the employee should share in the liability to third parties. In fact there is a widespread agreement between insurers and employers that these claims will not be pursued. This means that the damages system encourages too great a laxity about the actual causes of accidents, and it distracts from the important task of trying to discipline or punish those who are responsible for injuries and losses. The law is so concerned to see that the plaintiff gets his money that it does not worry overmuch about who pays it.

MORE STRETCHING OF THE PEOPLE YOU CAN SUE: PUBLIC AUTHORITIES

During the past fifty years there has been a huge growth of liability on the part of public authorities under the law of tort, but it is also in this area that in the past decade or so the judges appear finally to have decided to take a stand against some of the most extreme forms of stretching.

The first major development here was the passing of the Crown Proceedings Act in 1947 which rendered the state, or the government, liable to pay damages for the negligence of their employees in pretty much the same way as all ordinary employers. This Act does not apply to employees of other public bodies, such as the former nationalised industries, local authorities and so on. These public bodies are legally distinct from the Crown, or central government, and have always been liable for the negligence of their own employees, in the same way as ordinary companies. What the 1947 Act did was to extend this form of liability to the employees of the central government itself – that is civil servants and government officials. At first post office workers were also covered by the 1947 Act though now that the Post Office is a public corporation these liabilities have been hived off to that body; the armed forces were originally excluded from the 1947 Act but (as we note below) that too has recently changed. Later, other Acts have created vicarious liability for other public officials, not all of who were originally covered by the 1947

Act. For instance, since 1964 the local police force (in the person of the Chief Constable) has been vicariously liable for the acts of police officers.

The 1947 Act was at first hailed as a welcome gain for the small person against the Goliath of big government. When the Labour government of that time seemed about to turn Britain into a socialist state, so that more and more people were being employed by central government, many people thought it unfair and wrong that you could not sue the government for the negligence of these employees. Up to a point this complaint was justified, and in the case of ordinary everyday accidents (like motoring accidents) it is no doubt fair enough that the government should be liable in the same way as everybody else. If the law is a mess here, it was even worse before. But it was perhaps naive of lawyers to believe that you could simply equate the position of the government with that of ordinary businesses, though it has taken some time for the problems to begin to really show up. Recently it has become clear that the law must draw *some* distinctions between the activities of government and the activities of ordinary businesses. One obviously cannot have people suing the government claiming (for instance) that the Chancellor of the Exchequer has been so negligent in his economic policies that the plaintiff's employer has become bankrupt, and he has become unemployed. What is more, if the police services and the fire services and all other public services are to be judged as if they were ordinary businesses, they may find themselves held liable for negligence because they have not spent enough money on safety precautions – but "their" money is in fact taxpayers' money, and it is the government, representing the taxpayers which decides how much money they should have. Judges surely cannot be allowed to override government decisions about the allocation of money to public bodies.

In the past decade or two there have been numerous

cases brought against the government and other public
bodies which have raised some of these very difficult questions. One of the first main cases was the *Dorset Yacht* case
(about the escaping Borstal boys who damaged the plaintiffs' yacht), which has already been referred to (p. 51).
This was treated very much as an ordinary action of negligence in which the Home Office officials were held to be
negligent in allowing the boys to escape. But the case had
deeper problems which later began to surface. One of these
problems is that cases of this nature may involve policy
decisions by governments or other public bodies to whom
these policy decisions are constitutionally entrusted in our
system of government. If the Home Office decides as a
matter of policy that Borstal boys should occasionally be
allowed out on outings to encourage them to develop as
normal citizens, it is worrying if judges are then allowed to
declare that their actions amount to negligence because it
involves too great a risk to the public. Recently the courts
have become sensitive to this kind of argument and are
now more careful to avoid entrenching on these policy
decisions, but of course lower-grade activities or decisions
may still be judged to be negligent.

Another problem is the financial one, referred to above,
and more needs to be said about this in due course.
Judgments for damages against the government or other
public authorities have to be paid for by taxpayers, and it
might be thought that they have some real interest in seeing, therefore, who the money is paid to, and how much
is being paid. For example, police and health authorities
which now pay millions of pounds in damages every year
for the negligence or other torts of their employees are
finding their budgets depleted by these huge payments.
Every pound they pay in damages is a pound less available
for their ordinary tasks – preserving law and order, or the
treatment of other patients. In really bad cases a health
authority may pay out a million pounds for a single patient

– which of course means longer waiting lists, cancelled operations and all the rest of it, for many other patients. The question of priorities necessarily arises. Are parents who have suffered trauma and emotional disturbance, for instance, as a result of the death or injuries suffered by their children, morally entitled to half a million pounds if this means that really sick patients have to have their operations cancelled or postponed?

And what about huge damage payments by the police to members of the public who claim that they have been wrongly arrested? Because of traditional sensitivity shown to cases involving infringements of personal liberty, a person may recover many thousands of pounds in damages against the police for wrongful arrest, even if the arrest lasts only a few hours, even if he is completely unhurt physically, and does not even suffer any emotional trauma or shock. He is entitled to these large damages because his basic rights have been infringed – strictly these are not cases of negligence at all, but for our purposes they raise many similar questions. In 1995 the Metropolitan Police alone paid out £1.6 million in damages – nearly double the figure for 1990, and eight times the total ten years' earlier.[1] It is hard to believe that police malpractices have increased so much in these ten years – what seems to have happened rather is that more people sue and higher damages are awarded. And this is happening at a time when police resources are stretched as never before by the levels of crime. There is particular absurdity in these huge payouts in cases against the police, because this is one of the rare cases in which damages are awarded for the purposes of punishment – the law recognises that punitive or exemplary damages may be awarded in cases of this kind where the plaintiff's basic constitutional rights have been flouted in a flagrant manner. Unfortunately, since the damages are always awarded

[1] *Sunday Telegraph*, 1 December 1996, p. 9.

against, and paid by, the employers – that is the police authority, which in effect means the public at large – the wrong people are being punished. Individual policemen are rarely even disciplined for their behaviour in cases of this kind, let alone made to pay any of the damages. In early 1997 the Court of Appeal decided that exemplary damages against the police should not exceed £50,000, but they did not question the appropriateness of such awards.

As we have noted, the judges do appear to have decided finally to call a halt to some of the more extreme types of case in which it has been sought to render public authorities liable for damages for negligence. For instance, they have now overruled a series of cases in which local authorities were held liable to buyers of houses who found that their houses had been badly built, contrary to the local authority bye-laws. Local authorities, of course, employ inspectors whose job it is to ensure that buildings comply with the bye-laws, but inspectors are sometimes negligent, and may fail to notice breaches of the bye-laws which they should notice. At first it was concluded from this that the local authorities who employed the inspectors should be vicariously liable for these acts of negligence. These decisions have now been overruled, though mainly on the ground that the housebuyer's complaint is really that he has suffered *economic* loss only (even if the house is physically faulty, the actual loss to the housebuyer is the money needed to put the faults right), and this (as we have seen) is not normally actionable. But it might have been better if these decisions had been overruled on broader grounds, because it is not really obvious why the local authority should be any more liable if the housebuyer is physically injured by a part of the house collapsing on his head. Obviously the real responsibility for the bad construction in all these cases is that of the builder, not that of the local authority. But (as we have already seen) you can always sue *any one* of the people responsible for injuring you or causing you loss, and it does not matter that somebody else is *more* responsible. Since local authorities are always able to pay damages awarded against them, and are easy to find, lawyers prefer to sue them than to sue builders who may be small-time contractors without resources to meet a judgment, and who may even have disappeared or gone out of business.

The intelligent layman may well think that in this kind of case, more effort should be put into seeing that the real responsibility is met by the builders responsible, and the intelligent layman would be entirely right. But the law of damages is extremely uninterested in seeing that the parties really responsible for causing the damage should pay for what they have done, it is only interested in seeing that every effort is made to enable the injured party to recover from *someone*, no matter who. Fortunately, there have been some moves in the direction of placing liability on builders of new houses for faults in construction, through the National House Builders' Council, and that may well need further development. But for the moment anyhow, local authorities can breathe more easily over these cases.

Another very important decision of the House of Lords only last year[2] has put important limits on the possibility of actions against highway authorities for failure to eliminate or reduce dangers on or adjacent to the roads for which they are responsible. Although highway authorities can in principle now be held liable for failure to repair, this decision involved an attempt to make the authority liable for failure to *improve* the road in the interests of road safety, by removing a bank of earth which obstructed vision at a junction. It can be seen easily enough that if the law starts going in this direction, it is on a very slippery slope indeed – are we going to see judges decide that it would be negligent of a local highway authority not to build a new

[2] *Stovin v. Wise* [1996] 3 All ER 801.

roundabout here, or to install traffic lights there, or perhaps to turn a single carriage road into a dual carriage road? Yet, as we know, the sympathy of judges for injured accident victims, and their desire to see them compensated, are often so great that they are under constant pressure to find that *someone*, it hardly matters who, is liable for negligence. Fortunately, this decision appears to show the higher courts at least determined to leave these matters to be decided by local authorities, and not by judges, but it was a close run thing – the House of Lords' decision was only made by three judges to two.

Another important decision of the House of Lords in 1995 is now under challenge. In this case it was held that a local authority which fails to take children into care or otherwise protect them from abuse by their parents cannot be sued for damages by the children even if negligence is proved. The Official Solicitor is planning to take this case to the European Court of Human Rights,[3] which means that the taxpayer is paying the salary of an official who sees it as his job to try to force the taxpayer to pay damages to children who have been abused by their own parents. Truly, this is a Gilbertian situation.

The possibility of police forces being held liable for their *failures* (as opposed to ordinary acts of commission or positive acts of negligence) has also been firmly scotched by the courts. In 1988 the mother of a young woman who was murdered by the notorious "Yorkshire ripper" (who killed thirteen women and tried to kill another eight) sued the police for failing to arrest the ripper when (so she claimed) they had sufficient evidence to identify him long before her daughter was killed. Once again, it will be seen the police were not the actual parties responsible for the killings; the argument simply was that they had negligently failed to prevent the killings. The House of Lords threw

[3] *The Times*, 4 January 1997, p. 2.

out the claim,[4] holding firmly that the police could not be made liable in such a claim, even if they had been negligent. One of the main reasons for this sort of holding is that it is impossible to discuss what the police *should do* without having regard to resources. And here, as we saw earlier, it is important that judges should not impose their views on how much money public bodies ought to spend, because those sorts of decisions are constitutionally made in England by Ministers and Parliament. In the US where judges have traditionally wielded much greater powers than in England, judges have frequently forced local state authorities to spend huge sums of money (which they therefore have to raise in taxes) to improve standards in mental homes, prisons and similar institutions. This is one American road we do not need to go down. In England it is usually accepted that judges have no business telling Ministers or other elected authorities how much money they should spend (and therefore what taxes they need to raise) though it must be said that some recent decisions have got very close to doing this sort of thing.

All this does not mean that the police are not still liable for ordinary acts of negligence like careless driving, or, indeed, other torts like wrongful arrest, committed by policemen. What it means is that they cannot be made liable for failure to *prevent* crime, at any rate in the ordinary way, though in special circumstances (for instance if they know that a person is threatening the life of a particular individual) they may possibly come under a liability for failing to protect that person. If the courts allowed such claims for negligence more widely it is easy to see what a spate of litigation might follow. Have you been injured by a drunk driver? No matter, you could sue the police who ought to have stopped him. Have you been burgled? Perhaps you could claim for negligence because there was

---

[4] *Hill v. Chief Constable of West Yorkshire* [1988] 2 All ER 238.

no bobby on the beat. Have you been mugged? Perhaps the criminal was previously arrested and released by the police without charge, or let off with a caution – then you might be able to argue that they were negligent in not taking him before a court. Fortunately, claims of this kind are now unlikely to succeed. There may, of course, be difficult borderline cases, such as where the police respond to an emergency call but are so dilatory and inefficient in doing so, that a serious crime is committed which they could perhaps have prevented.

Things might have been worse still: suppose Parole Boards could be sued for negligently recommending the release of someone who goes on to commit more crimes? Or suppose (as happened in a case in 1996) that magistrates release a person on bail despite strenuous police objections and the accused proceeds to commit a murder – should the magistrates be liable for negligence? It seems safe to say that such actions would today have no chance of success.

It will be noticed that many of the difficult cases referred to above concern *omissions* to act by public bodies. Now it is paradoxical that the more things that governments do, the more frequently they try to protect the public from injury or other wrongs, the more likely it is that they will be criticised and attacked for not doing still more. If government public health authorities try to prevent the spread of infectious diseases, someone is sure to criticise them, and perhaps to sue them, for not taking steps earlier and more effectively to control a particular outbreak. If governments set up bodies to regulate and control fraud, in order to protect the public, they will certainly be open to criticism and often to legal action for not taking more effective steps to prevent fraud in a particular case. If governments establish fire services to put out fires, they will surely be criticised and perhaps sued for not fighting a particular fire more effectively, or putting it out sooner. If governments (or local councils) grit the roads in severe weather conditions, they will be sure to be criticised and sometimes sued for not gritting them sooner or in less severe weather conditions.

These may be quite natural reactions on the part of those who have been injured (as they think) by the failures of government or government-established bodies, but when governments take steps to protect members of the public against certain losses or injuries it does not follow that they should have to pay damages if their protective measures fail to work properly or efficiently. There is nothing absurd or unreasonable about setting up machinery to protect the public in various ways, while also refusing to compensate individuals who are injured or suffer losses when the machinery fails to work. In fact once it is appreciated that the damages system is fundamentally an insurance system (as appears more fully in Chapter 5) then the argument for holding the government liable for damages when their protective arrangements have failed to work, is seen to be, in effect, an argument that the government should provide free insurance to protect the public against losses and injuries. But there is no such thing as free insurance, so if the government is liable to pay damages, the public will have to pay for the insurance being given by the government.

So it must be understood that even when the government tries to protect the public against risks and injuries, these risks and injuries may still be the kinds of things people just have to learn to accept, unless they can protect themselves or their property, for instance by insurance or in some other way. Merely because the government provides a fire service, for instance, does not mean that the government is taking on responsibility for insuring houses against fires which they fail to put out. Merely because the government tries to prevent children from being abused by their parents does not mean that the public should have to pay damages to those children if they fail – though the

Official Solicitor wants to persuade the European Court of Human Rights otherwise.

Of course governments and government-established public bodies should not be immune from criticism for the way they have failed to use their powers in particular cases, but an action for damages is a very poor weapon for investigating whether public bodies have behaved well or badly. Because its main purpose is to compensate those who suffer injuries or losses the whole of the law becomes skewed to these purposes; and if the real purpose of the action is to investigate the efficiency of the body in question it cannot be done well by these means. Apart from anything else, payment may be offered to settle the claim out of court, and the worse the behaviour of the public body in question, the more likely it is that any liability will be met by such an offer of settlement. It is partly for these reasons, partly for more complex reasons perhaps, that judges are now beginning to acknowledge that there are great problems in expanding the liability of public bodies too freely in these negligence claims.

But many claims of this kind have still to be litigated and fought every inch of the way, often at great expense to all concerned. For example, problems have recently been raised about the local fire authorities, and are currently being litigated in a series of cases which may well eventually go to the House of Lords. Here the problems are slightly different from some referred to above, but the claims are even less meritorious. Because most fire damage is covered by the property owner's insurance, he will not normally be interested in claiming that the damage was worse than it should have been because the fire brigade was negligent in not putting the fire out quickly enough or in the most efficient way possible. But the property owner's insurance company is itself legally entitled to bring a claim in his name (under the doctrine of subrogation which is explained later, p. 131) and they may well be interested in suing the fire brigade, or strictly the local authority which employs the firemen, under the vicarious liability system. If many of these claims succeed the net result will be that a part of the cost of fire damage will be transferred from the property owners' insurance companies onto the shoulders of the local authority taxpayers. (Of course, in the process, a huge additional bill in legal costs will be incurred, so that if insurance companies recover say £10 millions a year, the bill for the local authority will be £10 million plus legal costs of probably another five or six million.) All this shows what happens when the legal system gets out of control. The wrong people will get compensated, the wrong people will pay, and only the lawyers will benefit.

The armed forces

As noted above, members of the armed forces were originally excluded from the right to sue under the Crown Proceedings Act of 1947, so that one member of the services was not permitted to sue the Crown (or the government, or the taxpayer, in other words) for injuries caused by the negligence of another member of the armed services – ordinary members of the public could sue, but not members of the services themselves. One very good reason for this exclusion was that members of the services injured on duty were entitled to pensions, as were the dependants of those killed on duty. But as the culture of damages grew, people began to question the immunity. Why should not members of the armed forces be entitled to the same bonanza as other members of the public if injured on duty? (One is reminded of the story of the young child who cried when shown a picture of ancient Christians being eaten by lions in the Coliseum, because one poor lion did not appear to have an ancient Christian to eat.) The inevitable consequence ensued, though in this case it was Parliament (supported by the public) which was to blame, not the judges. The Crown Proceedings Act was amended in 1987 by a private member's bill, to allow members of the services to sue for damages when injured by the negligence of another member. It is worth adding that the new Act does not deprive a serviceman who gets damages of his right to a service pension in respect of the same accident.

A small clause in the amending bill provided that the extra expenses incurred as a result of the bill by the armed forces (that is, the taxpayer) would be met out of sums to be provided by Parliament in the future. Members of Parliament were appalled when they were told what this actually meant. It was estimated that the cost of the Bill would be over £13 million *per annum*, of which almost half would go on legal costs. It was also estimated that twenty-four new lawyers would need to be employed by the Ministry of Defence to handle these cases at a cost (in 1987) of approximately £700,000 a year. That so many Members of Parliament were shocked by these figures is a shameful reflection on their own ignorance, since the facts about the legal costs of the damages system have been well known at least since the present writer's book, *Accidents, Compensation and the Law* was first published in 1970, and certainly since the Report of the Pearson Royal Commission was published in 1978. It is deplorable that the law was so lightly amended in this fashion on the assumption that the system of legal liability for damages is a fair and efficient way of compensating the injured.

In 1996 this change in the law led to a case being brought[5] which is surely entitled to the prize for the most undeserving damages claim of the decade (which is saying something). I will quote from the law report:

> "The plaintiff was a soldier serving with a British Army artillery unit during the Gulf War. While his unit was deployed in Saudi Arabia firing a howitzer into Iraq he was ordered by the gun commander to fetch some water from in

[5] *Mulcahy* v. *Ministry of Defence* [1996] 2 All ER 758.

front of the gun carriage. While he was in front of the gun the gun commander negligently caused the gun to fire. The discharge knocked the plaintiff off his feet and adversely affected his hearing."

So the plaintiff claimed damages from the Ministry of Defence (the taxpayer) for the alleged negligence of his gun commander in adversely affecting his hearing. In this war, it will be remembered, British service personnel risked, and in some cases, lost their lives. Casualties were, fortunately, very light, but there were some deaths and some injuries. Some airforce personnel were also captured by the Iraqis and suffered ill-treatment at their hands. Naturally, none of these people could claim damages because the Iraqis and not other British servicemen were responsible for the injuries and deaths. This was, moreover, a time when the British Army was a volunteer force, and did not include conscripts, so one might have thought that some degree of acceptance of risk was implicit in the mere fact of volunteering. Yet this claim for damages for adversely affected hearing was brought in an English court, and was permitted to proceed by a Circuit judge. Only in the Court of Appeal was the action thrown out on the entirely sensible ground that military personnel could not be made liable for what they did to other personnel in the heat of an actual battle. (Of course the action cost the taxpayer something anyhow, in legal fees for the Ministry of Defence, and possibly – this cannot be judged from the law report – for the plaintiff too if he had legal aid.)

The case deserves a little further thought. Why was it so easy to whip up enthusiasm for this change in the Crown Proceedings Act, when it could give rise to such absurdities? The answer, it has to be said, is because the promoters of the bill made good use of the procedure of *selective comparison*. When people are injured in accidents, *some* of them get damages. It seems unfair if those similarly injured in similar circumstances, can't get damages. So if an army lorry driver injures two people in an accident caused by his negligence, one of whom is a member of the public and one is another member of the forces, it seems unfair to some if the former can get damages and the latter cannot (even though the whole reason for this is that the latter gets a pension instead). But this argument requires a most amazing degree of selective comparison. In the Gulf War case referred to above our sense of fairness is surely profoundly affected by the comparisons we choose to make. We may say: this person has had his hearing affected by being unfortunately injured in an accident by the negligence of his officer; even though this was in a battle the officer should have been more careful; after all if this accident had happened back in England in a factory instead of on the battlefield, the plaintiff would have been entitled to damages. If we follow this line of comparison, the conclusion admittedly seems to be that it is unfair to deprive the plaintiff of damages. But we can draw a different set of comparisons, as I have tried to do above. We can say: this was a war, other people were killed and injured and captured, and none of them is entitled to damages. Why on earth should this plaintiff get any damages? Surely in a case like this, the second set of comparisons is more relevant than the first.

This process of selective comparison seems to be one of the driving forces behind much of the stretching of the law that has occurred. But it is a very odd process, statistically speaking. It always involves comparing a particular victim's position with that of others who are entitled to damages. But, for every one or two persons who recover damages, there are perhaps eight or nine others injured in accidents who do *not* recover any damages, and probably ninety others who are disabled or incapacitated from other causes who also do not obtain any damages. When comparisons are drawn for the purposes of a particular case, why do we not compare that case with others where the victims do *not* recover damages, since the great majority do not?

If when we are faced with a particular case, we compare the position of the plaintiff with those who are entitled to recover damages – the technique of selective comparison adopted by counsel arguing cases for injured plaintiffs, or by those promoting a change in the law to give more victims the right to claims damages – there will (it must be said) be no logical stopping point at all. Surely *everybody* who suffers from similar disabilities or incapacities ought to be compensated in the same way. But if there is one thing which is clear about possible reform, it is that society could not afford to compensate everybody who suffers disabilities and incapacities by the levels of damages awarded in tort cases. One glance at the figures given for the extra costs of the armed services amendment to the Crown Proceedings Act should be enough to show that. Quite what should be done is a question I address in Chapter 8. What I am concerned to do here is to suggest that the kind of change introduced by the "reform" of the Crown Proceedings Act is the wrong way to proceed.

HAS THE STRETCHING GONE TOO FAR?

It may be argued that things are not really as bad as I have made out. After all, in many of the most extreme cases I have referred to above, the claims have been thrown out by the courts. They appear to be trying to hold the line. So is there really such cause for worry? The answer is yes, there is. For one thing, as I shall show later, the whole system is built on such rotten foundations that even if we leave aside the more extreme and absurd claims now sometimes being made, there is ample cause for concern. The basic stretching of the law has already taken place and is far too deeply rooted to be eradicated by the judges. We have already moved so far from the simple idea of a morally guilty person being made to pay damages to a morally innocent person for his injuries, that the whole system is shot through with absurdity and unreality.

But some of the signs of further stretching that have been discussed in this and the previous Chapter are even more alarming – and it may have been noticed how many of them are very recent indeed. Even though some of the worst claims have been rejected by the courts, the very fact that these could be brought at all, often reaching the highest courts, and sometimes succeeding in lower courts before being rejected on appeal, is very worrying indeed. Many of these cases are brought under the legal aid system so the public is paying the high legal costs involved for the plaintiff, and often (where a public body is the defendant, as it frequently is these days) for the defendant too, where the claim eventually fails. What is more, many of the cases discussed here, though ultimately rejected, show the law still on a knife edge – the cases have often been turned down by appeal courts, divided three judges to two, or by appeal courts overturning a lower judge who has allowed the claim. The fact that lawyers feel these cases worth bringing suggests that there is a legal head of steam building up behind many of these claims, and it is known that other major cases are pending – such as those against fire authorities. Clearly, many lawyers feel that if they go on hammering at the doors long enough, more claims will be allowed, however absurd and extreme and farfetched they may appear to some.

Moreover, as we have already noted, the great majority of claims for damages never reach court but are settled by agreement in advance of a trial. When cases are settled in this way claims may well have a real nuisance value and lead to substantial damages being agreed even though they lie at the very frontier of legal liability. Defendants may be advised by their lawyers that no similar case has succeeded before, but the climate of legal opinion and the continuous pressure to expand liability may persuade them that there is a real risk of the case succeeding if it proceeds.

There is another worrying thing about the stretching of the law in these damages cases. The territory gained by plaintiffs' lawyers in cases they win is never (or hardly ever) given up; the arguments lost can be fought again and again, until some victories are permitted. In other words the frontiers of legal liability are always being pushed back. Occasionally a reverse here or there means the frontier is stabilised in certain types of case, while lawyers turn their attention to other cases, but it is very rare indeed for any of the territory so gained to be given up. There is only one major area of the law in which a significant retreat has occurred in modern times – the cases imposing liability on local authorities for negligent inspection of houses badly constructed by builders have been overruled. But the pressure for expansion of the law elsewhere is relentless. It is time to call a halt, and look back on what we have done.

4. WHO RECEIVES DAMAGES?

WE now need to ask who actually collects the damages paid out as a result of trials and settlements? In the past few chapters we have been discussing what the law provides, when injured people are *entitled* to damages. But being entitled to damages in legal theory does not necessarily mean that you will get them in practice. There is a whole range of factors which affects the question of who will receive damages in practice. One of the most important of these factors is the existence of adequate (or better) alternative ways of obtaining compensation, and we need to start with this.

Everybody knows that claiming damages is likely to be troublesome and possibly expensive, and certainly a long-winded process. Anybody who can claim compensation for his losses or injuries from other sources is likely to do so, in preference to claiming damages, unless he can get a great deal more money by claiming damages. Among other things this means that very few legal claims for damage to property (for example, damage caused by fire) are ever made or pursued. Since most property of any value is insured, and since claiming against your own first party policy for property damage is relatively painless and quick, there is rarely any point in claiming damages for property damage. What is more, you can't generally get more money by claiming damages in this situation, because most forms of first party insurance will pay you as much as you can get by claiming damages.

It is true that insurance companies can, and sometimes do, bring "subrogation" claims for the amounts they have

paid out in property damage first party insurance, so the
fact that the owner of the property can get his compensation easily and quickly from his own insurer does not necessarily mean the end of any possible claims (subrogation is
explained more fully later, p. 131). But by and large these
subrogation claims are rare compared to the amount of
property damage there is. Even insurance companies know
that in the long run subrogation claims which they win will
probably be balanced out by subrogation claims that they
lose. It is jokingly related that one insurance company,
having paid off its first party insured, tried to make a subrogation claim against the party responsible for a fire, only
to discover that he had a third party insurance policy
against that liability – and they were the insurers under that
policy too! Since they couldn't very well sue themselves,
they gave up that idea pretty quickly. So it is hardly surprising that claims for property damage don't figure very
largely in the statistics or the law books. And we can now
put them on one side as having very little statistical importance in the overall picture.

We shall also put aside here other claims which do not
arise from personal injuries because there is very little statistical information about them. Obviously, as we have
noted already, such claims may come from a variety of
sources – consumer claims, claims for breach of contract,
claims for bad advice and so on. But we know little about
the overall incidence of such claims. We can also put on
one side some of the more bizarre claims which have been
reported in the press in recent times, some of which have
been referred to in earlier chapters, such as the claims for
damages for being badly educated by incompetent schools.
Claims of this kind may well be worrying for many
reasons, but they still remain a small proportion of the
claims which are made every day and which fill the law
courts and lawyers' coffers. The overwhelming proportion
of these claims remain what they have been for about fifty

years, namely claims for injuries received in road accidents and in industrial accidents.

Even with these sorts of injuries many people will not make claims because they have simpler and easier forms of compensation at hand. As we have seen, there are basically three components to a claim for damages for personal injuries, (1) earnings losses, (2) medical and other health care expenses, and (3) damages for non-pecuniary loss, that is for pain and suffering and loss of amenities. Now very large numbers of relatively minor injuries produce no earnings losses and no medical expenses either. The reason why they produce no earnings losses is that large numbers of people in modern societies are anyhow not earners, but are housewives, or children, or students, or retired, or unemployed. Even among those who are earners, huge numbers of employed people are paid wages or salaries for short periods of sickness or injury – virtually anyone working in public service employment has the right to some months of sick pay, and many even in private employment will be paid something (if not full wages) when they are off work for short periods. Medical expenses are, of course, for most people taken care of by the NHS, so lots of people who suffer minor injuries simply have no significant financial losses to claim for at all. It is true that there remains the possibility of claiming for their non-pecuniary loss, but it is evident that many possible claims of this kind are just not made in minor cases.

There is some research on the reasons for this – probably it is due to a combination of factors, chiefly ignorance of the possibility of being able to claim for non-pecuniary losses at all, and a general reluctance to get involved with the complications of the law when the major problem of financial loss has already been taken care of. Sometimes, too, people actually blame themselves for their injuries, or at least they do not blame anyone else – it is only when they actually get to see solicitors and learn something about the law that they start claiming that somebody else was at fault.

CLAIMS FOR PERSONAL INJURIES

In the Report of the Pearson Royal Commission published in 1978 it was estimated that in 1973 (the last year for which we have such serious estimates) about 250,000 claims for damages for personal injury were made in the UK, of which about 215,000 were settled by some payment either by agreement or after a trial. Very few of the cases went to trial – only about one percent of them, though that still amounted to about 2,000 trials which in our legal system is actually a lot of cases, and of course, they cost the public a lot of money in judicial time and salaries. In fact most trials in the High Court *were* at that time personal injury trials. Still, the great mass of claims was settled in the way described in earlier chapters. Of this 215,000, almost ninety percent came from two sources only – road accidents and industrial accidents. Claims from a variety of other sources – medical injuries, other transport accidents, defective products and so on – accounted for the remaining ten or twelve percent of the cases. There is no reason to believe that very much has changed since 1973 though the total number of claims has probably gone up. There may also have been some slight increase in the proportion of claims from sources other than road accidents and industrial accidents (especially perhaps medical claims) but this is unlikely to have affected the total proportions by more than the odd percentage point here or there.

It must be stressed that of all the disabled or handicapped people in society, about ten percent suffer from birth defects, about another ten percent have been injured in accidents, and the remaining eighty percent are suffering from illnesses and conditions of natural origin. Of the total number, only a tiny minority obtain any damages at all –

the figure was estimated twenty years ago by the Pearson Royal Commission at about one and a half percent, and there are no serious later estimates. The position is illustrated in the following figure.

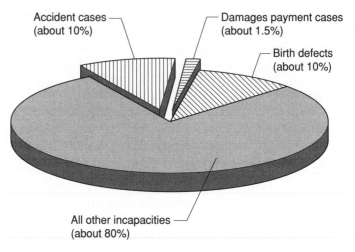

Cases of incapacity and proportion getting damages

We will comment later on the fact that such a tiny minority of injured and disabled people recover any damages at all (pp. 143 ff.). Here we need to tackle another question. Why do such a high proportion of claims come from road accidents and industrial accidents? Of course these are two of the main sources of accidental injury, but the accident statistics show that there are also very large numbers of accidents which occur in other ways – in the home for instance, and in other forms of transport besides road transport – and yet claims for these accidents are relatively rare. So too, many people suffer disabling conditions or diseases which may be attributable to someone's fault – industrial diseases, industrial deafness, and so on – and yet these too give rise to very few claims. Why should this be so?

The answer has little or nothing to do with justice, or which of the different possible groups of claimants most deserve or need financial assistance. It has far more to do with the characteristics of the legal system. In order to make a successful claim for damages, a number of hurdles have to be surmounted. Some of these we have already seen – you usually have to prove fault, and causation against the defendant. But there are a number of other factors which are also *in practice* requirements of a successful claim. These are, in particular, (1) that the claim must be provable, and (2) that the claim must be made against someone capable of paying the damages. In the two particular groups of accidents which give rise to most claims, road accidents and industrial accidents, these two practical problems are much more easily surmounted than in lots of other cases.

ROAD ACCIDENTS

We need to say a little more about road accidents. So many claims come from road accidents because these are among the easiest claims to make and to prove. This is not, of course, because those injured in road accidents *deserve* to be compensated more than those injured in other accidents – actually, as we have seen, a substantial proportion of these claimants are probably guilty of contributory negligence. It arises from the fact that road accidents are public affairs, and are the subject of a well regulated and standard set of police and other public procedures.

Road accidents involving injury must, by law, be reported to the police, and indeed in any serious case, the police are invariably called to the scene of the accident. They are trained to observe details, take statements and make careful notes, all of which will help a plaintiff who later wishes to claim damages. In the case of any serious injury, the parties affected will almost certainly be taken to a hospital casualty department. There they will encounter doctors and other medical personnel who are also trained in keeping careful records. All these are of the highest importance to the possibility of a successful claim being made. They provide independent evidence of the way the accident occurred, and the nature of the injuries suffered.

In addition to these factors, the law has made every effort to ensure that parties so injured will not be defeated by the inability of those responsible to pay claims for damages. Insurance against the risk of liability on the roads is compulsory, and every effort is made to enforce that legal obligation. It is treated as a serious offence to drive a vehicle uninsured, and you cannot renew your car excise licence unless you can produce your third party insurance certificate. And to catch the few cases where drivers flout the law, there is a special institution called the Motor Insurers' Bureau, set up by the insurance industry, under pressure from the government, to cover the liability. If anybody causes an accident on the road through his fault, and is not insured against that risk, the MIB (as it is usually called) simply takes over the responsibility for handling the claim just as though it were an insurance company, or it passes the responsibility to another insurer more directly involved, for example, a company which has insured the owner of a vehicle being driven without his permission. Still more special arrangements have had to be made for the case of the "hit and run" driver because in that kind of case, where the driver cannot be identified at all, you couldn't even begin to make a claim since you don't know who to claim against. And you couldn't sue him since you can't sue someone without first issuing a writ against him, and you can't do that if you don't know who it is you want to sue. All these difficulties have been got over by special arrangements with the MIB which accepts responsibility for these claims. The MIB draws its funds from the insurance industry, which in turn gets its income for these cases from the compulsory insurance which everybody is required to buy. What this means is that the law-abiding members of the public who do buy their third party insurance are paying for the claims made against those who don't.

Most people think these are very laudable arrangements – similar arrangements exist in many other countries, and in the UK they are the result of pressure by the government which has tried to make sure that road accident victims with good claims in law do not in practice go uncompensated. But although the motives behind these schemes may be laudable, it must be pointed out that the result is to create a highly privileged class of accident victims. Lots of other accident victims go uncompensated, lots of victims with good theoretical legal rights to claim, go uncompensated. Is it not odd, for instance, that a child injured as a passenger in an *uninsured* car by the negligent driving of its own father can claim damages against the MIB, while a child injured at home by the negligence of that same father acting quite lawfully, cannot? Is it not perhaps also odd that every law-abiding driver has to pay his share of the claims made against the MIB, while he has no claim against anyone if he unfortunately skids off the road, and hits a tree, and so injures himself even if the accident was not really his fault, but due (say) to unexpected black ice on the road?

INDUSTRIAL ACCIDENTS

The term "industrial accident" is here used in a broad sense to include all work-connected accidents, even though some of them may occur in offices or even on building sites rather than in industry itself. Like road accident victims, industrial accident victims are in many respects a privileged group. Here too, special laws exist to protect the victim and to make sure they can make claims for damages wherever there may be grounds for such claims. First, there are special laws requiring employers to take all kinds of precautions against industrial accidents; then there are special laws requiring such accidents to be noted and reports made to the Health and Safety Executive; then there are (as with road accidents) special insurance requirements, so employers must insure against their liability to their workers (though there is no MIB for work accidents).

In addition to all these provisions, those injured in work accidents often have the advantage of trade union assistance for any claims they may wish to make. One of the less known, but most valuable services that many unions provide to their members is to assist them to make claims for compensation where appropriate. This assistance is sometimes very generous, and may enable a claim to be made, or even litigated, without any fear of costs falling on the worker. Indeed, in some respects the unions may offer assistance which is actually more generous than that available under legal aid. Some unions have made a speciality of assisting their members for new kinds of claims; for instance the Police Federation have spearheaded many of the modern claims for post-traumatic stress.

The result is once again that large numbers of workers injured in industrial accidents do obtain damages, though it is still only a small proportion of the total number of work accidents which end with a successful claim.

We must now revert to our point about the practical difficulties of proof, because although claims arising out of industrial *accidents* may be relatively easy to prove, claims arising from industrial *diseases* are far more difficult to prove. Although it is widely believed that many serious diseases (including many forms of cancer and lung diseases) have some association with various forms of industry it is exceptionally difficult to prove the facts needed to support a claim. For one thing, these diseases often have very long latency periods – the illness may not manifest itself for twenty or thirty years after the exposure. By that time, memories have faded, work records will have disappeared, the industries or plants will have changed, managers will have been replaced, and the facts needed to support a claim may simply be unavailable. Then another difficulty arises from the legal need to prove causation. This commonly leads to a problem such as the following. The plaintiff is, say, suffering from bladder cancer. It is found that there is, on average, one bladder cancer case per 10,000 of population. Perhaps the factory where the plaintiff was working had three people suffering from bladder cancer in its workforce of 1,000. This is highly suggestive, but it is not necessarily proof, that the plaintiff's condition was caused by the conditions at his place of work. The result of all these factors is that claims for industrial disease are much less easy to make and much less common than claims for industrial accidents.

Workers' compensation

At one time, compensation for work-connected accidents (and some of the more common industrial diseases) was provided by a special system of workers' compensation. In the UK we had special workers' compensation laws between 1897 and 1948 which gave a right to claim compensation to anyone who was injured in an accident "arising out of and in the course of his employment." This compensation was not nearly as generous as common law damages, but it was provided on a no-fault basis, so that all workers injured in these kinds of accidents (or the dependants of those killed) could obtain compensation, and not just those whose accidents were caused by provable fault.

Most countries of the world still have no-fault workers' compensation laws, but in the UK they have almost disappeared. This has been the result of a rather strange piece of history which deserves a few words. In 1948 the Labour government introduced its new and very wide-ranging

National Insurance system which later came to be called Social Security. As part of this new system the former workers' compensation laws were in effect taken over by the new social security system, and became known as the industrial injury scheme. This was done because it was then widely thought that the workers' compensation system had become too adversarial and too court-based, and the trade unions wanted to remove it from the private insurance industry which at that time handled these claims, and transfer it to the state, which was thought perhaps likely to be a "softer touch". So there was a special system of state social security benefits under the industrial injury system, which was based on weekly payments, and of course these benefits were still provided on a no-fault basis.

But gradually over the years many of the special industrial injury benefits have been eroded. This has happened partly because governments, especially conservative governments, have been striving to cut the cost of the whole social security bill; and partly because it came to seem more doubtful if there was any real reason for paying better benefits to those injured at work than to those injured in any other accident, or indeed, to those incapacitated for work for other reasons altogether. In the world of social security the lawyer's distinctions between how accidents are caused seems largely irrelevant. These distinctions are of no importance to claimants of benefits, or to those who devise and administer the social security system – what matters to them is the degree of incapacity, not how it came about.

So the differential between the benefits payable to those injured at work and the benefits payable to other incapacitated persons has gradually been narrowed, although it is still true that anybody who is seriously and permanently affected by an industrial injury (or some industrial diseases) may be entitled to a benefit for life which other victims of accident or disease do not get. The result is that the unions now probably regret that workers' compensation laws were ever taken over by the state. Had they remained a responsibility of industry and private insurers, the government could have constantly increased the levels of benefits payable, while leaving industry to pay the bill.

At the same time, as the idea of workers' compensation laws has faded, actions for damages by injured workers against their employers have increased enormously, greatly assisted by the change in the law in 1948 which enabled one worker to claim damages from his employers for the negligence of a fellow-worker (see p. 75). All this has been a most retrograde development – the fault concept is well and truly back, the lottery is in full swing, more injured workers recover substantial damages, but most still get nothing more than bare social security benefits.

5. WHO PAYS?

THE GUILTY PARTIES DO NOT PAY

WE need now to look in a little more detail at a point
which we have already touched upon from time to time –
who pays for these damages claims? Again, we concentrate
here on personal injury claims. The first point, which has
already been made, and no apology is needed for making it
again, is that in serious cases the wrongdoers *never* pay. In
fact the only kind of case where the wrongdoers – the negligent parties – commonly pay are in very minor road accidents where a car is slightly damaged but no injuries are
caused. In these cases, reasonable motorists will often admit
their fault and pay out of their own pockets to save claiming against their insurance, with consequent loss of no-
claims bonus.

But in more serious cases, and in virtually all injury
claims, the parties guilty of negligence will not pay. In fact
solicitors acting for a plaintiff will not usually bother to
claim against them. They will simply extract the name of
the defendant's insurance company and address their claim
straight to the insurers. From then on, the whole procedure will be dealt with by the insurers on the defendant's
side, and the plaintiff's solicitor, on his side. The insurers
will decide whether to admit blame, whether to settle,
how much to offer, how to fight the case if it goes to trial,
what barrister to brief, whether to appeal if they lose, and
so on, all without even troubling to consult the nominal
defendant – the negligent party, or strictly we should say,
the allegedly negligent party. The late Professor Harry

Street, a leading expert on tort law, used to recount how he was once sued for injuries received in a minor road accident. In the first court the claim was dismissed, and Professor Street forgot all about it until he read in *The Times* some months later that the plaintiff had appealed and the appeal court had allowed the appeal and awarded damages against the professor, all without his knowledge! Of course the case had been handled by his insurers throughout.

Insurers may even choose to settle a case against the wishes of the insured who might prefer to defend it. In the recent case of the bullied schoolboy, for instance, the insurance company chose to settle the claim with a substantial payment against the wishes of the school authorities. The teachers of the school thought the action should have been defended, and (according to press reports) they were willing to give evidence that they had the problem of bullying under control, that the boy in question had never complained about bullying, and that they had seen no visible signs of serious bullying on the premises – in other words, that they had not been negligent. But third party insurance policies nearly always give the insurance company the sole right to decide whether a claim should be fought or settled, because the company has to pay the bill. So if this claim had been fought and lost, the insurers would have had to pay the costs as well as the damages. They made a commercial judgment that it was better for them to settle than to fight.

So damages are hardly ever paid by the people who lawyers call the "wrongdoers". Even in those rare cases where damages are awarded which are intended to be punitive – as in some cases for wrongful arrest and the like against police officers – they themselves will not pay the damages. It is, indeed, rare for them even to be disciplined by internal procedures in cases of this kind.

Some may think that, at least where damages are awarded against companies, the companies themselves are often seriously to blame and it is fair therefore that they should pay for their own faults. This is a very popular viewpoint, and we all tend to think of companies (and indeed other bodies like government departments or local authorities) as entities. "They did this" we say, and "therefore they should pay". Judges say it too, even in cases where the company is only vicariously liable for the negligence of its employees, and has not done anything negligent itself. But this is one of those areas where the popular viewpoint and the legal viewpoint both seem founded on misconceptions. A company or a government department or other public body is an abstraction. It is real people not abstractions who commit acts of negligence. Generally speaking, the liability of a company involves no imputation at all against the company itself – it is just legally liable for the negligence of its employees. Even where a company can itself be considered in some sense to have been negligent, where it has, for instance, allowed a sort of negligent culture to grow up, where the whole company is pervaded with the attitude that the public interest does not matter, that profits are their only concern, it is actual people who are responsible for this culture. When lawyers say that a company has itself been negligent, what they usually mean is that top management is responsible, but that does not alter the fact that the actual parties responsible do not pay for their faults. Who ever heard of top managers or directors paying for the consequences of their negligence? If anybody in the company is disciplined at all for acts of negligence it is unlikely to be the top managers or directors.

Paradoxically, there is actually one group of negligent people who do, in a peculiar sense, pay for their own negligence, and these are accident victims themselves. Whenever an accident victim who makes a claim has his damages scaled down because of his own contributory negligence he is paying, in a rather special sense, for his own negligence. People do not insure against the effects of their own contributory negligence so they "pay" for it themselves. If you are injured in an accident for which you are, say twenty-five percent to blame, and your full losses are £10,000, you will obtain damages of £7,500 against the defendant which his insurer will pay; but you will lose the other £2,500, for which no insurer will pay. You will yourself "pay", at least in the sense that you have suffered this loss and cannot recover damages for it.

Some people will probably find this very unfair; indeed, those who really believe in the existing system ought to find it unfair, because it does seem extraordinary that the only people who really pay for their negligence are accident victims. But, as we shall see later, accident victims who do obtain some compensation are actually treated so very generously by the law that it is hard to shed too many tears over those who have to pay for their own contributory negligence.

THE PUBLIC PAYS

If the actual wrongdoers don't pay for the damages, who does? The answer that has been given already is that, in a broad sense, the whole public pays. That does not mean that we should not care how the burden is actually distributed. It is actually very much like taxation. All taxes are, in the last resort, paid by the public, but of course the burden of taxation is not evenly distributed over the population. Some pay more and some less, and the way in which the burden falls is a matter of enormous public interest and debate. Again, we can see that the burden of paying damages may in the first instance fall on one group, but in the last analysis the burden may be passed onto another group. Let us look into this in a little more detail.

First, it is clear that businesses have to pay a large part of the cost of damages in the first instance. All large businesses insure against this sort of liability, and indeed, it is legally

compulsory for them to insure against their liability to pay
damages to their own employees. So in a sense, the damages will actually be paid by the insurance companies rather
than the businesses themselves. But of course insurance
companies have to collect premiums, and the business concerns who insure against this kind of risk have to provide
these premiums. Where do they get the money from to
pay the premiums? The answer is that finding the money
is just an overhead cost of the business, like the rent paid
for their premises, or the cost of heating the premises. The
business has to charge us – its customers – enough money
to cover its overheads, so some small part of what we pay
for all the goods and services we buy in the market is actually going to fund this kind of insurance, and ultimately to
pay the damages which the insurance companies have to
pay out. If the business is unable to pass on the whole cost
to its customers for competitive reasons then the shareholders (rather than, or as well as, the customers) will pay.
So damages premiums are just like a bit more VAT levied
on businesses, and passed onto the public.

There is a simpler, more direct payment route, with
regard to private motorists. As everybody knows, an ordinary motorist is legally obliged to insure against third party
risks – he has to buy insurance to cover the risk of being
held liable to pay damages through use of his car on the
road. So here again, the money is paid through insurance
companies, but is levied in effect as a charge on the
motorist. Since it is compulsory the resemblance to a tax is
stronger still. (The first party component of a comprehensive motor insurance policy is different – that is voluntary
and not compulsory, see p. 121).

In other cases the route through which the money
moves is even simpler, but the ultimate result is much the
same. For instance, whenever the government (or a government department) is held liable to pay damages, there is
no insurance because the central government never

insures, but the money is just paid for out of taxes. So here, it is even more clear that the damages are just like any other government expenditure which has to be paid from taxes. If the government wants to pay social security benefits, it has to raise taxes to pay for the benefits, and if it is willing to pay damages, it has to do the same.

THE CONSEQUENCES OF RECOGNISING THAT THE PUBLIC PAYS

The fact that damages are ultimately paid for like this, by members of the public, is critically important for a number of reasons. First, it means that sympathy for accident victims comes with a price label attached if we want to do anything about it. Sympathy itself is cheap; but if we want to translate that sympathy into more compensation or higher damages, then we, the public, will have to pay more. Some people may be willing to do this; others, looking at the huge damages sometimes awarded for relatively minor injuries, or in dubious circumstances, may feel less sure. About twenty years ago, when there were constant demands to improve the social security system and other welfare benefits of the state, it gradually was borne in on the public that these improvements had to be paid for by higher taxes, and since then the public reaction to these demands for higher expenditure has been more muted. A similar change does not yet seem to have taken place with regard to claims for damages. The public perception of these matters appears still to be that damages are somehow paid by wrongdoers, negligent and blameworthy parties, and this perception fuels demands for more and higher damages. It is time that the public understood that they themselves are paying for these damages awards.

Similarly, with government departments and other public authorities. Lawyers, and members of the public too, faced with an act of negligence committed by officials of, say, the Home Office, are apt to say: "The Home Office has been negligent, and the Home Office should jolly well pay damages for its negligence." Unfortunately, the law just does not work like this. The Home Office is an abstraction, or if your prefer, a building in central London. Neither abstractions nor buildings are capable of paying damages. If we actually spell out what happens in a case like this, we must say: "Officials of the Home Office have been negligent, so the public taxpayer should jolly well pay for it." This sounds a good deal less logical as well as less sonorous. So also, if the real employer is a group of shareholders, as with a public company, then demanding that the company should pay means actually that the customers or shareholders of the business must pay.

Acknowledging these realities may not change the public reaction very much. Many people would no doubt be prepared to go along with holding employers and public bodies liable for the misdeeds of their employees even though the parties paying are not the guilty ones. In the case of public authorities and companies, most people probably feel that the extra amount that the public have to pay to cover these damages awards is too small to worry about. And as to company shareholders, most people probably assume that all shareholders are wealthy, so there is not likely to be much sympathy for anyone who protests that shareholders are being made to pay for the negligence of company employees. All the same it is worth bearing in mind that about half of all shares in public companies today are held by pension funds and insurance companies, many of whose beneficiaries are actually widows and other dependants of those who have paid for their pensions or life insurance. So, if it comes to a sympathy battle between the injured accident victims and the companies, we should not automatically and instinctively side with the accident victims.

Still, it must be conceded that most people will probably think that companies and public bodies should pay for the misdeeds of their employees. Even so, the fact that the money is really coming from the public is vitally important for two other reasons. One is that it makes nonsense of the whole fault principle. Why should you only be entitled to compensation if you are injured in a fault-caused accident, when the money is really coming from the public anyhow? Nobody would set up a social security or welfare programme which only compensated those injured through the fault of others. Once it is grasped that the public is paying for the whole system, the basic structure of the system – the fault principle – becomes an absurdity. Remember that the identity of the person at fault is an irrelevance for practical purposes, and in some cases, is not even known. The contest is between accident victims who seek compensation, and the public, which will pay it. What relevance does it have that the injury is or is not caused by the negligence of some third party?

But the fault principle is not the only thing that becomes absurd once we see how close the damages system is to a tax or welfare system. It also becomes absurd to pay such generous sums to those who are entitled to damages, and nothing at all to anybody else who suffers similar (or even worse) misfortunes. The justification for the extremely generous way in which damages are assessed – full payment for all losses, past and future, no deductions, no limits, often duplicating other compensation receipts, damages for non-pecuniary loss, and all the rest of it – is that some guilty person (as we have seen, lawyers call him the "wrongdoer") is to blame for the injuries, and should pay in full for his fault. But once we see that he is not paying, and it is the the public who are paying, then this level of payments becomes, frankly, excessive. Just to take one example at this point, why should the public pay the huge income losses borne by the really wealthy – such as pop singers or tennis stars (see p. 9).

There is a third point of great importance which follows

once we understand that the public pays the damages. This
is that the public should surely have some say in how the
money is paid out, and how much is to be raised. Nobody
likes taxes, but at least they are levied by authority of
Parliament, and the public does have a chance to vote
every few years for MPs who these days are expected to tell
the public something about their taxing intentions. But
damages are levied by authority of the judges, they are not
subject to any parliamentary control or Treasury scrutiny,
and neither the judges nor anybody else really knows the
total amount being levied, whether it is going up or by
how much. Nor of course, does the public. The judges set
the benchmarks, and then the lawyers and insurance companies administer the system by settling most claims in the
light of these benchmarks.

There is rarely any informed public debate about this
system. Do we really want to pay high damages to fault-
injured victims (and only a few of those) and nothing at all
to others? Should damages be increased or are they already
too high? Even the government does not defend or represent the interests of the public on these matters. While the
government is a powerful guard dog of the public treasury,
and restrains increases in public expenditure because it
knows that these mean higher taxes, the government seems
indifferent to proposals which mean higher insurance premiums to fund higher damages. Law reform proposals
which have this effect are not properly scrutinised by the
government (nor by the Law Commission, which makes
them) and are indeed often treated as suitable measures for
private members' bills in Parliament. Yet the public is
effectively compelled to pay the costs of the system, very
much as it pays the costs of the social security system.
Premium payers as much as taxpayers need somebody to
defend their interests.

THE INSURANCE COMPANIES

As we have seen, insurance companies pay most of the damages awarded by courts or agreed in settlements. They also of course pay compensation to those who insure themselves against many ordinary risks of life. It is now necessary to explain more fully the central role which insurance companies play in the damages system.

The first thing it is necessary to understand is that there are two quite different kinds of insurance involved in the damages system, taken as a whole. One is third party liability insurance – which is just called liability insurance by insurance companies – and the other has no special name, but to distinguish it from third party insurance it can be called first party insurance.

Let us take first party insurance to start with. In this kind of insurance a person insures himself against a variety of risks. He may buy life insurance, which everyone is familiar with, although that tends to be rather different from most other forms of insurance in that death is a certainty, not a risk. However, death in a particular way (eg in a plane crash) or death before a certain date, or premature death is a risk which people often want to insure against and can insure against with life policies. Then there are first party accident policies of various kinds. When you buy comprehensive insurance for your car, that part of the policy which covers damage to your own car is a simple first party type of insurance. It is your car, you pay the premium, and if the car is damaged, you claim the cost of repairs from the insurance company. Nothing could be simpler or more straightforward. Householders' policies are also largely first party policies – you insure your house against the risk of fire, or the contents against the risk of burglary. Again, you pay the premiums and you collect the benefits of the policy if the risk occurs.

First party accident insurance is very common indeed

over property. Nearly all buildings are insured against fire, for instance. Not only is it a very sensible and prudent thing to have this form of insurance but when houses are bought on mortgage, the building society or other lender will insist that the house is insured. Most other valuable property is insured against damage or loss by theft, fire or other accident. Not all old bangers are comprehensively insured, it is true, but most cars of any significant value are so insured, and most other kinds of valuable property – jewellery, silver, gold items, valuable paintings or *objets d'art*, and so on – are also insured.

First party insurance is much less common in the case of personal injury. It may seem strange, given that the most valuable property you have is probably your own earning capacity, that it may not have occurred to you to insure it against the risk of injury. You would not really be to blame for that, because this kind of insurance is simply uncommon, most people don't buy it, the insurance companies have made little attempt to sell it until very recent times, and it is also rather expensive. What is more, many people probably believe (quite mistakenly) that their motor insurance somehow covers them against the risk of injury in a road accident, which is probably the most obvious risk of accidental injury that occurs to them. Until quite recently, most people have anyhow grown up with the idea that the welfare state will look after them in the event of catastrophic illness or injury, so they may well have thought it was hardly their own responsibility to worry about these risks. Furthermore, anybody who is a member of a good company pension scheme, or a public service scheme (which after all covers many millions of civil servants, teachers, policemen, local government workers, national health workers and so on) is usually given some measure of coverage against prolonged and severe sickness. Many members of these schemes will be entitled to sick-pay often for six months or more, and in cases of permanent injury, they will often be able to retire with enhanced pension rights. These are all similar to first party insurance in their effect, even though they may not technically amount to insurance.

Some people do have various kinds of personal accident insurance, strictly so-called, though they are usually limited in various ways. The best known are private medical insurance policies: if you are a "member" of BUPA you are actually insuring yourself against the risk of having to pay for certain defined medical or hospital costs. This is not the same thing, of course, as insuring your income. That kind of personal accident policy – where you do insure your income, or a part of it – is usually known as permanent health insurance, and it is commonly taken out by self-employed professionals, such as lawyers, doctors, architects and accountants. Heavy premiums have to be paid for this kind of income-protection insurance.

First party insurance

We can identify seven key features of first party insurance which differentiate it from third party insurance. First, there is one fairly obvious point. In first party insurance the person paying the premium is the person who stands to receive the proceeds of the policy if the risk occurs. This is actually a crucial point, because it is one of the ways in which the economic system best ensures the efficiency of the marketplace. When people buy things for their own benefit they can ask whether the benefits are worth the cost, they can shop around to get the best deals, and so on. When someone else buys things for you, you can never be sure the results will be so satisfactory.

Second, in first party insurance the premium varies according to the value of what is being insured. Obviously if you have a penthouse suite in Kensington it will cost you a great deal more in fire insurance than if you have a modest semi in Manchester. If you have a Rolls Royce your motor premium will be substantially higher than if you drive a modest Ford. If you want to insure an income of £100,000 a year it will cost you a good deal more than insuring an income of £20,000 a year, and so on. Nobody questions the fairness of this; it seems so obvious that it goes without saying.

There is a third obvious point about first party insurance – generally speaking this kind of insurance pays regardless of who is to blame for the loss or injury; indeed, often one of the main points of this kind of insurance is to protect the insured from the consequences of his *own* negligence. All comprehensive motor policies are designed to do that – we would hardly buy this sort of insurance if we couldn't claim for damage done in accidents for which we were ourselves to blame. Similarly, life insurance and health insurance policies don't refuse payment if the insured fails to take reasonable care for his health – by eating too much, for instance, or failing to take exercise. Some first party policies do include conditions which entitle the insurer to refuse payment in very extreme cases of fault on the part of the insured, and others may contain conditions (or demand increased premiums) for extra risks which are thought to be within the control of the insured; for instance life policies may require higher premiums from smokers, or may refuse payment to anyone dying of alcoholic excesses. And householders' policies may these days require householders to take reasonable precautions against burglary, or insist on installation of burglar alarms; holiday insurance policies often demand reasonable care of the belongings of the insured, and so on. But these are usually special and limited exclusions or conditions. In general, it remains true that first party insurance is "no-fault" insurance.

There is a fourth point about first party insurance that is very familiar. It rarely covers every penny of a possible loss. When we pay for our insurance policies we usually expect to cover part of the risks ourselves. Motor policies have excesses, and the no-claims bonus system makes it not worth while claiming for trivial losses even over and above any excess. Holiday insurance often contains exclusions for the first £100 or the like. Permanent health insurance nearly always pays benefits only after a specified period, usually three or six months' incapacity for work, and then usually only insures a proportion of the income lost. The reason for this is that covering every penny of a loss by insurance is usually too expensive; it is silly too, because it costs a lot of money to administer claims for tiny sums, and in a reasonably affluent society many people can bear small losses themselves.

Fifth, first party insurance hardly ever offers benefits as wide in scope as can be obtained in a claim for damages. For instance, claims for pain and suffering and loss of amenity are almost never covered by first party policies, though some limited accident policies like holiday insurance may offer specified sums for a few defined injuries – so much if you lose an arm or a leg, or are blinded, and so on. Property insurance is always, of course, just an indemnity against the cost of buying a replacement, and often does not even cover the cost of replacing old belongings with new ones – though some policies do offer this uplift. Personal accident policies, health policies and so on, are usually designed just to cover real financial losses, medical costs or income losses.

Sixth, first-party insurance is optional. Whether you buy it, and how much you buy, is normally up to you. It is never legally compulsory, though it is true that in the case of householders' insurance the practical effect of a mortgage may be to make it virtually compulsory so long as the mortgage lasts.

Seventh, in first party insurance the maximum sums for which the insurance company is liable are either fixed in advance, or are at least defined within reasonably fixed limits. Insurers who cover the risk of fire on a house know roughly what the value of the house is; life insurance is usually for a fixed sum, and though these days there are often with-profits policies the amount to be paid under such a policy is within the control of the insurance company. Property insurance usually states the value of the property or at least states what the property is so that its value can be assessed within defined limits.

Third party insurance

Third party insurance differs very substantially from first party insurance in all these ways. Let us first get clear what exactly a third party policy is, and who is the mysterious third party referred to. A third party insurance policy is a policy under which the insurance company agrees to indemnify you, the insured person, if you are sued or held legally liable for injuries or damage done to a third party. You are one party, the insurance company is the second party, and the person you injure who claims damages against you is the third party. On the face of it, it is similar to ordinary first party insurance. You pay a premium to protect yourself against a risk – namely the risk of being sued. But in reality this kind of insurance differs greatly from first party insurance, in all the above seven ways.

Many important kinds of insurance policy have both third party elements and first party elements. A comprehensive motor policy, for instance, is both a first party policy (insofar it covers your own car against damage or theft) and a third party policy (insofar as it covers your potential liability to pay damages to third parties). What is very often not appreciated, however, is that the first party component only covers your car, not you yourself. Nor does your third party component cover injury to you yourself, because you are not a third party – you can't sue yourself under your own policy. Your third party policy covers everybody in the world except yourself. However, one of the quirks of the whole system is that though *your* policy doesn't cover you, you may be covered by somebody else's policy if you are injured through his fault. Just as your policy covers everybody else, but not yourself, so everybody else's policy covers everybody (including you) except the policy-holder himself.

We can now look into the differences between third party and first party insurance. First, then, in third party insurance the person who actually gets the benefit of the policy is in reality the third party, not the insured person. The insured person is only nominally the beneficiary of the policy. In most cases he could not pay the damages awarded against him if they were not paid by the insurance company so actually the policy is very little benefit to him. In practice the money is always paid direct by the insurance company to the third party (or his solicitor) and does not even pass through the hands of the insured person. Among other things this means that with third party insurance the insured person does not choose the kinds of benefits he wants to insure against – he just buys the policy and pays for it, but it is the law which settles how much is to be paid to the third party if he makes a claim.

Second, in third party policies the premiums do not vary with the value of what is being insured, in fact they can't, because what is being insured is a potential legal liability, and it is not possible to know in advance what that liability will be. Now this has very important results. As we saw before, it is the most natural thing in the world that the owner of a Rolls will pay more to insure it than the owner of an old banger; but we can now see that this only applies to the first party component of an insurance policy. So far as the third party component is concerned there is no special reason to charge the owner of the Rolls more. This also goes, perhaps even more importantly, for income losses. If you have a first party permanent health policy insuring your income against loss, the more you cover, the higher the premium will be – obviously and fairly. But income

loss is not covered by the first party component of road
traffic policies, it is only covered by the third party component. That means that motorists do not pay premiums
which vary with the incomes they may stand to lose. This
has very dramatic consequences on the way the costs of
motor insurance are borne. A person with a very high
income who is seriously injured in a road accident may
recover enormous damages for his lost earnings, and if he
is killed his dependants likewise can recover a very substantial sum. But a person who earns much less will recover
much less, and a pensioner (or an unemployed person)
who is not earning at all, will recover nothing for his lost
earnings – yet the premiums he pays for the third party element of his motor policy do not reflect this. He pays just
as much for this element of his insurance as the high
income earner. There is no justice in this.

Next, third party insurance, unlike first party insurance,
is almost entirely fault-based. This follows from its very
nature. To claim under a third party policy you have to
claim damages against the insured party, but you can't usually claim damages unless he was at fault. Now although
the fault system has been stretched almost to breaking
point, it cannot be denied that in many cases an injured
person still cannot obtain compensation because he must
be able to prove that the injury occurred through someone
else's fault as the law understands that term. Because most
road accident injuries occur in collisions, in which both
parties are often partly to blame, this means that probably
half of all personal injury losses occurring on the roads are
simply not covered by insurance. The extraordinary result
is that, while most vehicle damage on the roads is covered
by first party insurance, a large proportion of personal
injury losses is not covered at all.

The position is even worse with regard to other accidents. It is, actually, much easier to prove fault in the case
of road accidents than in the case of most other accidents;

and in addition to the need to prove fault, the need to prove causation also presents acute difficulty in many cases such as where the plaintiff suffers a serious occupational disease which he says was the fault of his employer. The upshot of this is that, in principle, third party insurance just covers far fewer risks than first-party insurance. If you insure your house against fire, you don't expect to receive compensation only if the fire was caused by someone else's fault – that would be a totally inadequate form of insurance; likewise with comprehensive motor insurance; likewise with life insurance. In all these cases, first party insurance is in principle extensive in its coverage, and does not require proof of fault. Yet most personal injury cases do require proof of fault.

Having to prove fault not only greatly cuts down the coverage and hence the utility of insurance, it also adds enormously to the cost. In most first party insurance claims, lawyers are quite unnecessary. You don't need a lawyer to claim under a life insurance policy – it doesn't need a lawyer to prove the insured is dead. Nor do you usually need a lawyer to claim under comprehensive motor policies, or indeed any other first party insurance policy. But it is virtually impossible (or anyhow, very unwise) to make a third party claim without the aid of a lawyer. Now as we all know, lawyers do not come cheap. All professional services are expensive, and lawyers perhaps more than most. Third party insurance swallows up a huge amount in legal and other administrative costs. In 1978 the Pearson Royal Commission estimated that at that time some £200 million a year was paid out in damages in tort claims, the vast bulk of which was paid under third party policies. The cost of making these payments was no less than £175 million. In other words, for every pound paid in insurance premiums to cover third party claims, about 53.3 pence goes to pay damages, and about 46.7 pence goes to pay the lawyers' fees and other costs. This monstrous expense is absolutely built into the present system, and cannot just be put down to lawyers' greed. If you need to prove fault, and you also need someone to explain what damages you can claim, then you will have to have a lawyer. And if you have to have a lawyer someone must pay his fees. What is more, if you have to have a lawyer the other side may have to have a lawyer too. Actually, in many serious cases, a considerable additional part of the cost comes from the medical fees of the consultants and other expert witnesses needed to assess the extent of the injuries, and what long-term effects they are likely to have. And these consultants' fees have to paid too, so it is facile just to blame the lawyers' greed for these costs. It is the whole system that is wrong and rotten, not the lawyers who do their best for their clients within the existing rules.

The next distinction between first and third party insurance is that first party insurance rarely covers every penny of a loss. Everybody is familiar with excesses and deductions under insurance policies of various kinds. There are good reasons for these excesses and deductions, which are designed to minimise the number of small claims. Minor claims are disproportionately expensive to administer, because obviously any insurance company must check the claim against the policy terms, whether the claim is for £10, or £100 of even £500. And if any correspondence ensues between the claimant and the company, it takes just as much time and money, whether the claim is for a very trifling sum or a more substantial amount. So it makes good sense to have deductions and excesses. It is in the long term interest of consumers as clients of insurance companies to have them, otherwise they would certainly pay more for their policies. In fact some kinds of insurance, like motor insurance, offer as optional extras, ways of cutting down on the excesses, like insuring to protect your no-claims bonus – of course there is nothing wrong with this if clients are willing to pay the extra costs involved, as indeed some do, but many prefer to take the risk of minor excesses and deduction rather than to pay extra premiums for this sort of protection.

Third party claims have no such deductions or excesses, because they arise from claims at law, claims to which the plaintiff has a legal right. If you cause some minor scratches to your own car, you may decide it is not worth bothering about having it repaired even if you are comprehensively insured, (especially if the car is a few years old), because of the excess and possible loss of a no-claims bonus; but if you can claim against some other person responsible, and hence against his insurance company, you will probably have the right to have your car resprayed at their expense. Of course so long as we live under the present system you are entitled to do this, and nobody can blame you for claiming your rights. But a different system would save us all money in the long run. Most of us would probably prefer a system under which (if we wanted to) we could pay less for our insurance, and put up with a few minor scratches to our cars. Perhaps we would prefer to do that with regard to injuries too. At present, the slightest injury entitles you to make a claim – the bus driver starts up too soon as you board a bus, and you fall, grazing a knee slightly, and perhaps tearing your tights. Write a letter of complaint to the bus company and you may find them (or their insurers) offering you a trifle in compensation for fear of a much bigger claim. Or trip over a paving stone and write a complaint to the local council; the result may be the same although any injury may be totally trivial. Of course, we all have to pay for these costs in the long run. Do we really want a system that entitles people to claim for every such injury? Isn't the inevitable result going to be to encourage people to bring groundless claims, to pad and inflate them, and hope to screw a hundred pounds out of the system here or there?

Much the same goes for the next distinction between

first and third party claims. Third party claims cover a much wider range of types of injury and "loss" if that term is appropriate. Damages for pain and suffering and loss of amenity are the chief example of extra types of claim which can be brought under a third party policy, but hardly ever under a first party policy. Once again, it is we, the public, who pay for all these claims, thus inflating the costs of our insurance premiums, and some of the taxes we pay, as well as the costs of many of the goods and services we buy.

The sixth distinction between first and third party insurance, is that generally speaking first party insurance is optional, while much third party insurance is compulsory. It is true that as a practical matter, you often don't have a great deal of choice even with regard to first party insurance – as we have seen, you will have to insure your house if you have a mortgage, you virtually have to buy first party insurance if you buy a package holiday, and your employer may compel you to join the company pension scheme which may contain life insurance and other insurance-type benefits. But even in these cases there is often some degree of choice (for instance as to the amount of insurance you want) and there remain other kinds of first party insurance which are truly optional. Comprehensive motor insurance is entirely optional, permanent health insurance, and BUPA-type medical insurance are optional, householders' contents policies are optional, life insurance is generally optional, and so on.

Third party insurance is, however, often compulsory. And it is compulsory in two different ways. First, it is of course compulsory in the way most of us are familiar with if we own a car – it is legally obligatory to buy insurance against third party risks. But third party insurance is compulsory in quite a different sense too. It is compulsory in the sense that you cannot choose whether to opt in or stay out of the existing law regarding claims for damages. You cannot, in other words, say: I will happily waive my claim to sue others if they injure me, in return for not being liable to be sued if I injure them. That may sound a very strange idea at first, but if we had a choice, many of us might actually prefer to "opt out" of the law of legal liability, and then buy first party insurance for our own protection, as far we felt we needed it.

Some of us might find that quite a tempting idea. For a start, we could probably cut our insurance bills quite a lot by doing so. Then we could concentrate on protecting what we really want to protect, and perhaps not worry about damages for trivial injuries, or pain and suffering and loss of amenities and so forth. Certainly, many of us would probably prefer to insure ourselves on a no-fault basis. Those of us who are retired could stop paying premiums to insure our incomes, since these will continue whether we are injured or not. . . . It is a dream world, of course, because we have no choice. We *have* to join the present scheme or system, we *have* to pay the subscription, even though we don't like the rules, and think the subscription is much too high to be worth the benefits it brings us.

Finally, third party insurance is rather unpopular with insurance companies, as compared with first party insurance, because they never know the maximum amounts they will have to pay under third party policies. A third party policy requires the insurance company to cover the whole cost of *any* legal liability that may be imposed on the insured person, and that falls within the terms of the policy. If the judges decide to go mad, and double the level of damages to be awarded next year, the insurance companies will still have to pay the whole lot, even though their premiums are inadequate to cover the increased liability.

In the case of claims for personal injury, road accidents and the like, this is not actually a serious problem in the UK, because the levels of damages are well-known, do not usually change without adequate warning, and are anyhow quite low by the standards of insurance company activities. But even in personal injury cases the problems can be very serious in America, where damages are much more unpredictable, and in other kinds of cases, the problem is serious even in the UK because of the size of possible claims against accountants and solicitors, as well as in a variety of other contexts.. The result is that in cases of this kind, insurance companies now write in maximum sums for which they will be liable in their policies. One of the worrying types of case where these maximum sums get written in are cases of massive oil pollution and the like, caused by spills from oil tankers. Hundreds of millions of pounds of damage can be done in these cases, and the insurance is often inadequate to cover all the liabilities. Special arrangements may well be needed for cases of this kind which are too specialised to be addressed in this book.

So far we have been discussing the differences between first and third party insurance as though these were always alternatives. Actually, there is often a great deal of duplication in the insurance market, because many risks are covered by third party *and* first party insurance as well. Take the everyday case of a road accident which causes damage to your car, but does not injure anybody. The risk may be covered by your own comprehensive policy, but it is also very often covered by someone else's policy. Whenever the accident is the fault of somebody else driving on the road, his third party policy should also cover the risk. So the risk is covered twice. Of course, as everybody knows, it is beneficial to you to claim against the other driver rather than against your own policy if you can; but it is only beneficial because of the system under which we live. And the system brings in its wake increased cost. Suppose in this simple collision, both cars are damaged, and suppose both cars are comprehensively insured, and suppose both drivers are partly to blame. The result of this everyday type of case is that each driver is entitled to claim part of the cost

your own company can make the claim *in your name but on
their own behalf*. As lawyers put it, they are subrogated to
your rights, that is to say, having paid your claim, they take
over all the rights you had to claim against the third party.
In some cases, large sums of money turn on this doctrine.
Whenever property of any value is insured, and damaged
or destroyed by the negligence of another person who is
insured (or is otherwise worth suing), the first party insurance company, having paid off the owner of the property,
can then claim the amount from the negligent party, who
will in turn rely on his (third party) insurer to defend the
claim and pay the damages if he loses. In the *Dorset Yacht*
case, for instance, (above, p. 51) the plaintiffs' yacht was, as
is usual and normal, insured, and the owners' insurance
company paid for the damage. That insurance company
was responsible for launching the claim against the Home
Office, which being a government department did not
insure, but met the claim itself. So, having received a premium to cover the risk of damage to the yacht, the plaintiffs' insurance company was nevertheless able to pass the
cost onto the Home Office. But (as we have noted already)
an action against the Home Office is really an action
against the taxpayer. We see then that the official title of
the case, *Dorset Yacht Co.* v. *Home Office*, is actually a decep-
tive misnomer. What the claim was really about was
whether yacht owners and yacht club members or taxpayers should cover the damage done to yachts in circumstances of this sort. When this reality is understood, many
people may revise their ideas about the justice of the claim.
But the law conceals the reality in this kind of case. Judges
decide these cases as though the contest really *was* between
the yacht company and the abstract entity known as the
Home Office. Very often, subrogation claims are not only
brought by an insurance company, but are also brought
(effectively) *against* an insurance company. Because the
Home Office, as a government department, does not

insure, there was no third party policy in the *Dorset Yacht* case, but if they had been insured against liability, the whole action would have been fought between two insurance companies. These actions bring no benefit to the public at all, though they inevitably cost a great deal, and there is a good case for total abolition of insurance companies' rights of subrogation.

In the case of personal injury (as distinguished from property damage) claims, there is no subrogation and the law is different. Here, any insurance policy you have yourself is disregarded when you claim damages from the other party and get it from his insurance company. That means that you *do* get paid twice over in these cases. So, as we have previously noted, any life insurance policy is disregarded in a fatal claim, and any private pension rights you may have are disregarded if you claim damages for being unable to work. Naturally, once a person is injured in an accident, and goes to his solicitor to launch a claim, he will claim what the law entitles him to, and nobody can blame him for doing so. But most of us would be a lot better off if these duplicated claims were not allowed. Take the problem of life insurance in particular. Lots of people have life insurance policies. If they feel their families need protection, they can buy whatever they feel they need and can afford. And if they work in a company or a public body which has a good pension scheme, there will almost certainly be benefits payable to widows and dependent children if the employee is killed, or even if he dies through illness before reaching pensionable age. People who buy these life policies or who are members of pension schemes are, of course, paying for these benefits one way or another. And they may well not *need* any additional life insurance. But the third party insurance system forces them (in effect) to buy and to pay for this additional life insurance element. When you buy your third party motor insurance policy you are paying for *other people's* life insurance, should you kill them in an accident;

and when they buy their policies, they are in turn paying for *your* life insurance. So there is no escape – you *have* to have this additional element of life insurance, and obviously you have to pay extra for your third party policy because of it. But of course it isn't anything like as useful to you as ordinary life insurance, and you can't rely on it to justify not taking out ordinary life insurance, because the third party life insurance will only help if you are killed in a fault-caused accident, and then only if it occurs in a way covered by the type of policy in question. So the upshot of this complicated story, is that in personal injury cases, there is a wasteful duplication of life insurance protection which everybody has to pay for.

The differences between first and third party insurance which have been summarised above should suggest that first party insurance is, in most cases, infinitely preferable as the way to cover the risks of most injuries and losses, at least so far as they affect consumers, and often in other cases too. It has a broader coverage, it is far cheaper to administer, it allows some degree of choice, it saves money for the benefit of all by eliminating trivial and duplicated claims, and it imposes the cost of the premiums on those who have more valuable things to insure. Yet so long as we are lumbered with the present system of tort liability claims, we are compelled to use third party insurance rather than (or sometimes in addition to) first party insurance to cover our risks. The present system is a mess.

WHO PAYS IN CONTRACTUAL CASES?

Contractual cases are generally outside the scope of this book, but we have seen that there are some claims for damages for negligence which are classified as breaches of contract, and raise issues very similar (if not identical) to those which arise in other negligence actions. It is worth adding a few words about these cases because it is possible to identify who pays for these claims in contractual actions quite precisely, and also because they constitute a different group from those who pay for other negligence actions.

Where liability for negligence arises in contractual cases, contracting parties are likely to insure against that liability just as they do for other negligence actions. But whereas in ordinary cases the cost of this insurance is likely to be passed on to the general public as we have seen, in contractual cases, the cost is likely to be passed onto the very customers who are protected by the right to sue. Let us illustrate the point by looking at a case which came before the courts in 1995. The case concerned a holiday in China sold by a tour operator to the plaintiff's daughter. Various excursions and trips were organised by the tour operator as part of the holiday, and on one such trip, where a party of tourists were being ferried across a lake, the speedboat carrying them capsized because it was being negligently driven, and the plaintiff's daughter was tragically drowned. The plaintiff was held entitled to damages for her daughter's death on the ground that the tour operator was liable for the negligence of the operators of the ferry even though these operators were not employed by the tour operators, but were independent contractors. Now it is plain that if tour operators are held liable for injuries and deaths occurring in this way either they will have to insure against the risks, if they do not already do so, or their premiums will go up, if they do already do so. (This increase will not be because of the particular accident record of the tour operator, but because the insurers will have learnt from the court's decision that they are being expected to cover a wider risk than they had previously thought.) Naturally, if the tour operator's premiums go up, they will have to charge more for the holidays they sell, and the customers will pay more. Is that a good thing? The answer is no, because almost every holiday maker who buys a package holiday is already covered by first party insurance. This means that the holiday maker will be paying for two lots of insurance, and even though he can sometimes claim twice over for one loss, who wants that kind of insurance? So it is almost certain that holiday makers would be better off without this "right to sue" which they will be compelled to buy as a result of the court's decision whether they want it or not, and whether they need it or not.

Take another illustration: photographers who take or send their films for processing are sometimes indignant to discover that their films have been accidentally lost or destroyed by the film laboratories. The film processing companies usually offer to replace the films, but customers often feel that this a wholly inadequate form of redress. Some years ago a family from Australia, on a holiday trip round the world, took scores of films for processing to the Kodak laboratories where they were all unfortunately lost. The family threatened to sue Kodak, demanding that Kodak pay them the cost of having their holiday all over again, so that they could take their films a second time. The claim was settled by Kodak who paid a very large sum to the family, if not quite enough for them to have their second holiday. In 1996 a scientist who had taken a single film to Boots for processing, sued Boots for £30,000 damages for its loss, claiming that the film had been taken in the arctic on a scientific expedition which it would cost this huge sum to duplicate.[1] Now if processing companies have to pay large claims for damages like this, they will inevitably pass the cost on to their customers, so the result must be a substantial addition to the cost of film processing. Those whose films contain nothing more exciting than photos of their children or the family dog will have to pay extra so that those who holiday round the world, or who travel on scientific expeditions to the arctic can replace their valuable photos. (But if they are really so valu-

---

[1] *The Times*, 10 December, 1996, p. 1.

able, why don't the scientists take a few extra films to be on the safe side?)

Consumers are apt to sit on the sidelines cheering these David v. Goliath battles, and thinking that the claimant is representing consumer interests. Actually claims like this are usually quite contrary to consumer interests, because consumers will only end up paying more for their purchases. If these risks were covered by first party insurance rather than legal liability and third party insurance, then those who have specially valuable films to protect could be left to buy special first party policies, while those who do not, could save themselves the extra expense. Ideally perhaps, the film processing companies should offer to arrange this sort of insurance at a modest extra cost for those who want it – rather as the Post Office offers you the choice, at an extra cost, of posting valuable packages by registered mail or recorded delivery. This is obviously a more sensible procedure than making the Post Office liable for lost packages as a matter of law, which could only lead to an avalanche of claims, and a consequent increase in postal costs for everyone.

6. AN UNJUST AND INEFFICIENT COMPENSATION SYSTEM

In this chapter we shall draw together some of the threads and try to assess how well the present law works. So far as personal injuries are concerned, the whole legal-insurance process amounts to a compensation system, but a system which is unfair, and also exceedingly inefficient. But we will begin with a broad question about the "blame culture" and ask whether this is something contrary to the public interest.

THE LAW ENCOURAGES THE BLAME CULTURE

Many members of the public feel uneasy about the increasing spate of claims for damages, and one of the problems they are able to identify, without having any technical knowledge of the law, is that it encourages people to blame others for their misfortunes. This encouragement takes two distinct forms. First, the public are encouraged to think that others are responsible for taking the necessary precautions to prevent accidents or misfortunes occurring, and secondly, they are also encouraged to think that it is the responsibility of others to take the necessary financial steps (by insurance or otherwise) to safeguard them against loss when these misfortunes strike. There can be no doubt that the legal system, as it operates today, is partly responsible for this. The legal system is helping to create a 'blame culture" in which people have a strong financial incentive to blame others for loss or death or injury.

Some may argue that this is to put things the wrong way round. The legal system, they may say, is simply responding to public demands – if a blame culture has grown up, the law and the judges are not responsible for that, but must indeed respond to it, by offering redress to those who are able to show that others really are to blame for their injuries or losses. Of course, there is some truth in this too; the fact is that the law and the public culture or ideology react upon and influence each other. But it cannot be denied that the law has played a major part in creating the present blame culture. In particular, the "stretching" of legal liability in so many different ways which is itself largely the product of the insurance system backing legal liability, has diverted attention from the need for first party insurance. It is, for instance, amazing and entirely unacceptable, that the risk of damage to vehicles in road accidents is more extensively insured than the risk of personal injury (above, p. 124).

Governments are particularly vulnerable to litigation when the "blame culture" gets out of hand. If the public thinks – as some people seem to think – that ultimately the government is responsible for everything that happens in society, then the government (and other public bodies) are liable to get sued, whatever they do or fail to do. Take for instance, the problem of advice which in modern times the government is expected to provide on many public health issues, from drugs to contraceptive pills, to how much alcohol it is safe to drink and so on. Governments are always under great pressure to give advice on these matters: the media, professing to act on behalf of the public, demand to be "told" if it is safe to eat beef or to use a particular brand of contraceptive pill, and so on. If the government refuses to give this advice, the media claim that the government is "concealing" information which the public are entitled to have. And the government can be threatened with legal action for "failing to warn the public" of dangers. So the government takes scientific advice and passes it onto the public with its own recommendations. If the advice turns out to be wrong the government is again liable to be sued – in fact legal action is now pending on the advice over "safe beef".

Yet what has the government done wrong in these matters? It does not compel people to eat beef or use particular drugs or drink what the government says is a safe level of alcohol. These are matters on which it might be thought the public should make up their own minds, and accept responsibility for their own decisions. It is partly a result of the blame culture that the public think that the government should be responsible for what people eat or drink simply by giving advice on these matters. Perhaps the government's mistake is that instead of simply passing on the recommendations of its scientific advisers and advising the public to make up their own minds, it has framed its messages to the public in terms of categorical advice or assurances about safety. But in a culture in which the public was more accustomed to accept responsibility for their own decisions and behaviour, the government might be entitled to claim that all this should be so obvious as to go without saying.

There are some signs today that the law and some of the judges may have got out of phase with a changing public mood. The blame culture appears closely related to much of the ideology and the culture that dominated the country in the 1960s and 1970s. At that time it was common to blame the government for most of the social ills the country suffered from. If only the government would spend more money on this or that – hospitals, schools, roads, pensions, the police, social security and the rest of it – the public seemed to think, society's problems could be solved. Governments themselves often seemed to share this attitude.

In the last decade or two public attitudes to these questions, and certainly government attitudes, appear to have changed pretty fundamentally. It is now insisted by the government, and appears to be largely accepted by the public, that there are very real limits to what governments can do to solve all these social problems. In particular, any real attempt to solve them all by the government itself would involve an enormous increase in taxes, and anyhow might not work for a variety of reasons.

Once this comes to be accepted, inevitably what will follow is a greater stress on the idea that individuals must accept responsibility for their *own* problems. If the state cannot pay generous enough pensions to enable retired people to live in comfort, then people are going to have to learn to save more for their own old age. And if they don't do that it will be increasingly accepted that they are *themselves* to blame for their poverty in old age. Or again, if the state cannot afford to pay for (say) all dental treatment for the entire population, it must come to be increasingly understood that people are responsible for paying for their own dental treatment, and if they fail to look after their teeth, it will be *their fault*, and nobody else's.

Now, although the public mood may have changed with regard to social security and the welfare state generally, this change of mood does not yet appear to have affected the idea that claims for damages are something to be encouraged in the belief that others will always be paying the bills for these claims. The way in which MPs in 1987 flocked to support the private member's bill which allowed service personnel to sue for damages (as discussed above on p. 89) illustrates how badly informed many politicians are on these issues. In modern times it often seems that some judges are also caught up in the culture which was perhaps dominant on these issues in the 1960s, and are inclined to allow people to blame others very readily for their injuries or losses. We have already seen some vivid examples of this kind of thing, such as the case of the widow of the naval airman who choked to death in a drunken stupor, and yet was able to persuade the Court of Appeal that he was only partly responsible for his own death, so she was able to obtain £70,000 in damages (above, pp. 40–41). Judges are often some twenty or thirty years behind the times when it comes to the public mood and matters of ideology, but in the past this has generally led to criticisms of the judges on the ground that they are too conservative. Paradoxically, on this issue, it could be said that they are still too much under the influence of the vaguely left-wing welfare culture of the 1960s, even though both major political parties and the public itself have now moved away from it.

Yet the law of damages is closely related to the public problems of social security, pensions and so on. If the public comes to accept that it is *their* responsibility, as much as that of the state, to ensure they have adequate pensions when they retire, perhaps they can also learn to accept that it is *their* responsibility to insure themselves against the risks of injury and accident and so on. Few people would today expect to get an income for life – at the level they would hope to earn if they were working – when they are unable to work for any reason. It is, indeed, clear that we have already moved into a new social era when people are already realising that permanent jobs for life are not there for the taking for every school-leaver or university graduate. Many of these young people know full well that, out there in the real world, there are many risks which will influence whether they will have a decent job and income. Redundancy and unemployment are familiar phenomena for large numbers of people, and the fear of them perhaps even more familiar. In that kind of world, it will surely come to seem more natural that a person should be responsible for insuring, or otherwise providing against, the risk of income loss through accidental injury, rather than expecting others to provide the insurance cover, through the legal system, for this sort of risk. If that happens it will come to seem very strange if the law continues to make such generous provision (even allowing for some "discounting", see p. 10) for damages for "lost" future earnings, for damages in fatal cases, and indeed, for the whole idea that someone else should pay for our own insurance benefits. Judges themselves may begin to change their minds about what is just in these matters.

Some people may object that, although the blame culture may sometimes go "over the top", we do actually need to blame people where they really are to blame. We may need to punish people who are seriously blameworthy, and even where punishment is not justified, we may need to deter people from conduct which causes injury or accident. This is a point which we must not ignore, but the present emphasis of the law is so much on the awarding of compensation to the accident victim, that it actually tends to distract attention from the need to punish or make accountable those who are genuinely responsible. Although the "blame culture" may lead to more claims being made, once the claims are made, the whole effort of the law is bent to securing monetary compensation for the victim and not to punishing the blameworthy parties. We will return to the question of punishment and deterrence in Chapter 7.

THE SYSTEM IS A LOTTERY

We turn now to discuss the fairness and justice of the law insofar as it operates as a compensation system for personal injuries. How fair is the system? The answer is that the system is about as fair as a lottery. In fact it is not too much to say that it *is* a lottery, a lottery by law. It is almost a matter of chance whether you can obtain damages for disabilities and injuries; it is almost a matter of chance who will pay them; it is almost a matter of chance how much you will get. Just look at the facts.

We have already seen that of all the disabled or handicapped people in society about ten percent suffer from birth defects, about another ten percent have been injured in accidents, and the remaining eighty percent are suffering from illnesses and conditions of natural origin. Of the total number, only about one and a half percent apparently obtain any damages at all. How is this tiny group selected for preferential treatment?

Perhaps we should first say how they are *not* selected. They are not selected on the basis of *need*. Of course it cannot be denied that serious accident victims who obtain large damages often do need a good deal of money to cover their basic living costs and other necessities. But a disabled or handicapped person who does not come by his injuries in an accident may have similar needs, and that does not entitle him to damages. Some, of course, have more need than others, depending on the nature of their handicaps, on their age, and on whether they have good family support, or need to look after themselves and pay for their own support. These things do not decide whether you are entitled to get damages, either. Again, accident victims who can claim damages are entitled to the cost of private hospital, medical and nursing care. Of course they won't get these costs unless treatment is needed. But this entitlement does not depend on proof that *private* treatment is needed. Other victims may have a greater need for private medical treatment for one reason or another, but that is irrelevant.

Nor does the entitlement to damages depend on *how serious* your injuries or handicaps are. Obviously, injuries, illnesses, and handicaps vary enormously, from the truly terrible paraplegic cases of completely bedridden patients, to the trivial scratches or bruises which many suffer in minor accidents, or relatively trivial handicaps arising from natural causes, such as a minor sight defect that is remediable with glasses. But whether you can claim damages does not depend on how serious your condition is. The system is, of course, heavily biased in favour of accident victims because, as we have already seen, it is much easier to prove negligence in these cases, and it is also much easier to find an insured or solvent defendant. And because of this bias there is a tendency to assume that the most seriously handicapped people are usually the ones who have been injured in accidents. But this is not necessarily true. Even though much ordinary disease is no longer life-threatening, and modern medical science can perform miracles with many patients who would formerly have died, the fact is that there are still many terrible diseases and conditions which leave people with appalling handicaps, for which doctors can do little except alleviate pain. There are, for instance, the victims of birth defects like cerebral palsy (sometimes known as spastics); there are the victims of multiple sclerosis, and motor neurone disease, which are dreadful progressive paralytic conditions for which there is no known cure; there are sufferers from diabetes which can be controlled by daily injections of insulin, but which often leads to serious complications in later life, frequently requiring amputations of limbs (and most limb amputations, it should be noted stem from disease and not from accidents); there are those suffering from spina bifida, another congenital condition but one which is not caused at birth but is due to inherited characteristics. Many of these are very serious conditions – and of course there are others too – which can be heartbreaking in their effect. Many of them are far more serious than injuries for which damages are often obtained.

Nor do your chances of obtaining damages depend on whether the condition is *permanent or temporary*. After all, minor injuries, and short term sickness are part of the human condition – virtually everybody has such injuries and illnesses at some time or another. The great majority, fortunately, prove short-lived and leave no permanent ill-effects behind them. But whether you can claim damages or not does not depend on whether your illness or injury is short- or long-lived, it does not depend on whether it leaves any ill-effects behind it. Even the most temporary and trivial incapacity can legally justify a claim for damages, and though the damages will be modest in such a case, when all these claims are added up the total cost may be considerable. Of course most people won't make a claim for trivial short-term injuries like this, but some do.

As advertising by lawyers grows, as the "blame culture" flourishes, and public awareness about these matters grows we can expect a greater "claims consciousness" as the Americans call it, and more claims for minor and even trivial injuries. Already some people have discovered how easy it is, for instance, to make claims against the local council's highway department if you trip over a protruding paving stone on the pavement and graze your leg; and trade unions often encourage their members to claim for very minor industrial injuries.

Next, as we have also seen, your ability to claim damages does not necessarily depend on *how innocent* a victim you are yourself. It is true that if you are wholly to blame for your own injuries you won't be able to claim anything; (though if you are to blame for injuring your wife *she* may be able to recover damages) but you can still obtain very substantial damages if you are partly or even mainly to blame. On the other hand, lots of the most innocent victims of all – for instance children born with birth defects – cannot recover a penny.

Now that we have seen what your entitlement to claim does *not* depend upon, we can ask, what it *does* depend upon. We can answer this very shortly here because we have already largely covered this point. What it does depend upon, is, first, whether your injuries or condition are due to the fault of another person; secondly, whether you can *prove* this; and thirdly, whether the person who is to blame is insured against that liability or was acting as an employee of a company or public authority when the injury occurred.

There is often a considerable element of chance even

about these factors. For many disabled or handicapped people the effects of their disabilities are precisely the same however they were caused, and it is in one sense pure chance whether they were caused by someone's fault or not. Take, for instance, birth defects. As a disabled child grows up, not of course remembering anything about the events which caused its disabilities, it may seem the purest chance whether the child will be one of the very few who can recover damages for them. We have seen, too, how injuries which most people would call accidental can be blamed on someone else, and damages recovered against him, if he has through his fault just triggered off the events which occurred, even though nobody could have foreseen the result (see p. 46). Again, these results seem entirely fortuitous.

There is certainly a huge element of chance over the requirement of proof. As we have seen (p. 104) this is often very difficult or even impossible in many cases of industrial diseases; but it is much easier in cases of accidents. This is just luck. Even in cases of accident, it may be a matter of sheer luck whether witnesses are available, and therefore whether the cause of the accident can be proved. There is also pure chance involved in family cases – whether a spouse or child can recover for injuries which are the fault of another family member will almost always depend on whether the accident occurred on the road or elsewhere.

The second and third requirements of a successful damages claim tend to mean that whether you can claim will also very often (though not always) depend on whether the accident occurred on the road or in your work or in some other way. If it occurred on the road or at work, your chances of being able to get damages are much higher than if the accident occurred elsewhere. These two requirements are very much matters of chance, which have nothing to do with the guilt or blameworthiness of anyone else, or the innocence of the plaintiff.

Some of the mass claims we referred to in Chapter 1 raise this lottery point in an acute form. There are, for instance, about 120,000 tobacco-related deaths annually in the UK. It is obvious that if the families of all these victims received damages at anything like the normal rates, (about £100,000), the total cost would be astronomical – of the order of £12 billion annually. Clearly this is never going to happen – Parliament would change the law if it looked like happening. So the lawyers handling these claims must be hoping and planning to obtain damages for some of them rather than all of them. But which will be the lucky families? The answer must be that those who can hope to recover will be the ones who can *prove a case*, for instance, because the victim always smoked the same cigarettes, and suffered from a rare form of cancer which was nearly always associated with tobacco. Other victims won't have any real chance of success.

The lottery element in the system extends not only to whether you can claim at all, but also to how much you will get. Many people who are injured or suffer some serious medical condition, can get financial assistance from the welfare state in one form or another, so it must not be assumed that they will be left without resources altogether if they fail to get any damages. But it is well known that the welfare state is increasingly tending to become a bare safety net to help those without any resources; people will look in vain for generous handouts for social security or other welfare benefits for injury and disease. By contrast, those who can claim damages are given Rolls Royce treatment. Every penny of loss is carefully calculated by expert (and highly paid) doctors, consultants and rehabilitation experts. Expected future losses are calculated too. Something extra for pain and suffering and loss of amenities is thrown in. And (as we have noted above, p. 70) there is often a substantial duplication in entitlements so those who recover damages (especially in fatal cases) are sometimes better off financially after the accident than before.

Even with the detailed calculation of damages, some matters are still largely governed by chance. The assessment of future losses is, as we have seen, obviously a very difficult problem in many serious cases. It must be decided by the judge (or in a settlement) how the plaintiff's work prospects will be affected, whether he will be out of work, and for how long in the future this will continue. Naturally, despite all the care in the world, these estimates will often prove quite wrong. In some cases the plaintiff will be under-compensated because his work prospects will turn out to be worse than expected; in others he will be over-compensated because things will work out better than anticipated. When a judge decides, for instance, that a 35-year old plaintiff who has suffered post-traumatic shock will never work again, and awards him huge damages to cover a life time's loss of earnings, one can only wonder if this prediction will prove true. Indeed, if the prediction does not prove true there is a further lottery element in that the outcome may turn on chance timing. If the plaintiff recovers before or very shortly after a decision is reached, it may still be possible for the decision to be undone, and the damages reduced as happened in one major case in 1996 (see above p. 11). But if the recovery only starts a few months later this will not happen.

The basic lottery element is that, in one sense, it is almost pure chance whether an injured person ends up with damages or only with social security benefits. At the time of the Pearson Royal Commission Report in 1978 it was estimated that of all the money spent in compensating injured and handicapped persons, including the damages payments, the social security costs, and the administration costs of these systems, the one and a half percent of victims who received damages got about forty percent of the total; while the remaining ninety-eight and a half percent of victims had to share out among themselves the other sixty percent. Does anything further need to be said to demonstrate how unfair the whole system is? Yet there are still people who believe that the levels of damages should be increased! Indeed, at the time of writing the Law Commission was currently preparing several Reports which were thought likely to recommend such increases.

If anyone suggests that, after all, there is nothing wrong with a lottery, and that the national lottery is very popular, so why should the legal system not rely on the lottery idea, the answer will surely be apparent after a moment's reflection. Taking part in an ordinary lottery is a voluntary activity; being injured or disabled, and therefore involved in attempts to obtain compensation, is not. At the same time, it would only be a slight exaggeration to say that it would be no more unfair if all the available money at present paid out to victims of accident and disability were distributed by random selection like the lottery winnings. It would certainly be a great deal cheaper.

Who pays for all these damages depends almost as much on chance as who receives the money. It is true that in a sense we all pay, as this book has shown; but the proportions in which we pay are very varied, and seem to have very little relation to the risks we create, the amount we stand to obtain in damages if we are injured, or any other rational criteria. High earners pay no more than low earners, or the unemployed, but obtain far more if they are injured. Shareholders in companies held responsible for major disasters may end up suffering substantial losses, but are no more guilty of wrongdoing than anybody else. Local authority taxpayers may find themselves sharing a part of a bill for damages awarded against their authority for the negligence of an official over whose conduct they had no control. And so on. It is like taxation, but worse.

THE SYSTEM IS INEFFICIENT

Sometimes justice has to be sacrificed to efficiency. It is often expensive to design a really just system of laws, and we may have to do with second-best in some areas because of the cost. But the compensation system that we have today is not only unjust, it is very inefficient too. This inefficiency takes two main forms – the system takes too long and it costs too much.

Delays

First, too many claims take far too long to process. This is not due to delays caused by log-jams in the courts. As we have seen, only about one percent of these cases are ever tried; but the ones that are settled also take far too long. In serious cases, claims often take six or seven years to settle, some cases take even ten or eleven years – in other words longer than the Second World War. About half the claims take more than a year to settle. People who work the system, like solicitors and insurance companies, get used to these delays, and so tend to test the speed at which claims should be dealt with by what they are accustomed to. But other kinds of insurance claims – first party claims in particular – don't take nearly so long to handle. Life insurance payments are usually made within weeks; comprehensive motor claims are usually dealt with as soon as arrangements have been completed for the damage to be repaired; householders are often agreeably surprised at the speed with which insurers can deal with a major disaster. Why should it take so long to handle injury claims?

There are several reasons. One is that claims like this are made under the third party insurance system. The insurance company is not dealing with its own client, but with a stranger. It knows nothing about him, and owes him nothing for customer loyalty. So insurers may be dubious or sceptical about such claims, at any rate in the first instance.

Another reason, which affects serious cases, is that until the plaintiff's medical condition stabilises it is impossible even to try to assess what damages should be agreed. But this reason in turn depends on an unstated assumption –

namely that the damages must be awarded in a single lump sum. That being so, of course, it is often necessary to wait until the medical condition has stabilised, which may take years in a bad case. If damages were paid in periodical instalments, week by week as losses occur, the first payments could often be made very quickly. As we have noted before (p. 14) it is now sometimes possible to get something paid on account, by way of an interim award, but these awards are far from being routine.

A third reason why it often takes so long to process these third party claims is because of the need to prove that someone was legally responsible for the damage or injury. This is a much more complicated question than usually arises in first party insurance claims, because of the need to prove fault. As we have seen at some length, in straightforward cases fault may be a simple matter, though even when simple in law, the facts need to be *proved* – or at least there must be evidence to support them, in the form of statements from witnesses, documentary evidence and so on. Gathering this evidence may well take time even in simple cases, and whenever more complex issues arise, of fact or of law, things obviously become a great deal more difficult and time-consuming.

The upshot of all these factors is that long delays in the processing of these claims are absolutely standard, all over the world. Nor is it any use thinking that tinkering with judicial reform is going to make much difference since probably ninety-nine percent of the claims never go to trial anyhow. What might make a difference is converting the present insurance system from a third party system into a first party system, and eliminating the need to prove fault. We return to that possibility in Chapter 8.

Cost

We have already mentioned how costly the third party personal injury system is to operate. The Royal Commission estimates (which were given above (p. 125)) were that something like £200 million were paid in damages, at an administrative cost of £175 million, during the years 1971-1976 (the figures are at 1977 price levels). There are no up-to-date figures showing what the total cost is today but it cannot be much (if at all) short of two billion pounds annually, of which a little over one billion is being actually paid out in damages, at a cost of a little under one billion in expenses. Bear in mind that these costs are being borne by us – the public – just as certainly as we bear the burden of taxation for (say) the social security system.

These figures may not seem so huge when set against the enormous cost of the whole social security system, which today runs at something like eighty billion pounds a year. But they certainly are very large figures in themselves; and what is more the costs of administration of the damages system are far higher than the costs of administration of the social security budget. Most social security benefits are disbursed at a cost to the public of around ten to twelve percent of the sums paid out. If the sums paid out as damages could be disbursed in this same way the public would save perhaps £700 million a year. Because public bodies are generally and widely believed to be far less efficient than private ones, this may seem surprising at first sight. But it is the natural result of the complexities of the damages system which account for the extra costs of administration just as much as they account for the delays in the processing of claims. When you have to employ lawyers to handle these claims, costs are going to be high.

In this connection, it is worth remembering that at the time of the amendment to the Crown Proceedings Act in 1987, which allowed service personnel to sue for damages for injuries, it was estimated by the Ministry of Defence that they would need to employ twenty-four extra lawyers to handle these claims (see p. 90). If the Ministry had to employ twenty-four lawyers to defend the claims they expected to be made against them, then it is reasonable to assume that the service plaintiffs would also have had to employ the equivalent of twenty-four lawyers to make the claims. So this one apparently minor amendment to the law – this little extension of the right to claim damages – was expected to provide work for forty-eight new lawyers! One wonders how many new lawyers are being employed as a result of all the "stretching" of the law described in Chapters 2 and 3! Indeed, to say "one wonders" is strictly correct, because there is no way of knowing how much this costs. As we have pointed out already, these changes in the law are made by the judges without any estimate of the extra cost to the public of what they are doing. Perhaps Treasury scrutiny of public expenditure is not such a bad thing after all, if it protects the public from wasteful expenditure of this kind.

HOW HAVE WE GOT INTO THIS MESS?

In one sense it doesn't matter how we have got into the present mess. If it is a mess – an unjust and inefficient mess, as has been demonstrated – then the important question is what should we do about it, and that question is addressed in Chapter 8. But some people may be sceptical about these claims. They may think this book exaggerates, or is biased. They may think it is impossible that things can be as bad as suggested here. They may, in particular, wonder how if this account is accurate, things could have got so bad without anything being done about it. This section is addressed mainly to those who may ask themselves, how have we got into this mess?

The answer probably lies in a number of different factors, none of them particularly discreditable to the legal system or those who operate it. The answer does *not* lie in some gigantic legal conspiracy. The system has not been devised by lawyers to line their pockets, still less by the judges to line the pockets of their former colleagues. Actually the system has hardly been devised by anyone – it has just tended to develop bit by bit, from some very simple ideas, as we saw in Chapter 1, starting from the basic point that if somebody injures you through his fault he should compensate you. Most of those who operate the system are convinced that it is basically a just system which enables injured people to recover damages with their assistance against others who have committed wrongs against them. They do their best for their clients within the rules.

Nor does the answer lie to any great degree in the greed of those who may sometimes appear to be falling over themselves to claim damages. Perhaps the system does encourage this kind of response; certainly, when there is a lot of publicity about strange claims and large settlements or verdicts for apparently undeserving plaintiffs, many others may feel tempted to try their luck with the system, even though they would not otherwise have done so. The worse the system gets, the greater this problem will become. And it is also true that the system encourages injury victims to exaggerate their symptoms, whether consciously or unconsciously. But at present most people who claim damages are probably not motivated primarily by greed. They may have needs, or they may have grievances. If they go to solicitors to advise them they tend to get caught up in a system they do not understand. Solicitors assume that complainants who come to them seek what the law offers them – the right to damages. And once the machinery of the law creaks into action, it tends to follow a predestined groove. So we should not blame the people who operate the system or (in general) the people who take advantage of it to claim what they are entitled to. The real trouble lies elsewhere.

What has gone wrong is probably due to five main factors. The first is the resolute refusal of the judges and the legal system to face the fact that the wrongdoers who are actually responsible for the injuries that get compensated, do not themselves pay the damages. But even this is not due to any blinkered refusal to face reality. It actually originated in a rule of procedure in the days when civil actions were tried by juries that the plaintiff was not allowed to mention the fact that the defendant was insured. The purpose of excluding the insurance element from consideration was originally to make sure that juries were not biased against the defendants. Judges thought that juries would too readily sympathise with injured plaintiffs if they knew that insurers were going to pay the damages Paradoxically, this book has argued that excluding the insurance factor from consideration has in the long run powerfully assisted the stretching of liability, rather than the reverse. Now that judges try these cases they know perfectly well that the damages are going to be paid by insurers anyway, even if the details are concealed from them, so they have no fear that awarding large damages will bankrupt some poor defendant who has just made a mistake. At the same time, refusing to discuss insurance has meant that every action for damages appears to be a contest between an innocent plaintiff and a negligent wrongdoer. In such a contest, sympathy will always be with the plaintiff.

A second factor, closely related to the first, has surely been the powerful tendency which most people have, and which lawyers and judges share, to treat groups of people as entities capable of being held responsible for the wrongdoing of any one of them. The huge growth of the principle of vicarious liability, and the modern treatment of public institutions, has surely followed on from this. It is so easy to call a group "they" and say that if a member of a company or a public official does something wrong, "they" should be called to account and pay damages, that few of us stop to ask if this form of reasoning is really justified.

The third factor which explains the way the law has spread is surely the process of selective comparison which we referred to previously (p. 91). Whenever counsel is arguing a new type of case on behalf of a plaintiff, and is seeking to persuade the judges to "stretch" the law a little, he compares the instant case with the closest one to it, in which damages have previously been awarded. The whole system of precedent encourages this procedure. Judges are readily persuaded that the difference between the present case and the last one is too small to have any real weight, so the law is stretched – again and again and again, as we saw in Chapters 2 and 3. Defending counsel rarely have the same success in persuading judges that the instant case should be better compared with other cases in which no damages have been awarded – possibly for the simple reason that most of these other cases never get to court at all, and do not therefore constitute precedents.

Precisely the same thing seems to happen even when reform of the law is considered. The Law Commission, for example, has recently published a consultation paper about damages in personal injury cases. In this paper the Commission spends many pages learnedly comparing the way damages are assessed in many other countries with the way damages are assessed in England, but nowhere does the Commission look into its own backyard in England to compare the way damages are assessed with the sort of compensation made available to those unable to obtain damages at all. An afternoon spent with the clients of a local authority social services department or occupational therapy department will quickly reveal many victims of injury and disability who receive no damages and are assisted out of very meagre budgets indeed. These cases get little publicity compared to cases which end up in the High Court, so it is the latter which are always chosen for purposes of comparison and which the public get to hear about.

A fourth factor is the growth of paternalism and the blame culture, which among other things has led many of us to attribute blame for injuries and accidents and losses to others, when we ourselves are perhaps responsible for what has happened, or at least could have insured against the risks. When people start, in all seriousness, suggesting that insurance companies are responsible for advising their clients how to spend the money that is due to them under pension plans, and should be liable to them if they fail to give them this advice (see p. 49), we can see how far paternalism and the blame culture have got.

Closely associated with this fourth factor is a fifth. The law has been so taken up with developing a satisfactory system of third party insurance to cover the liabilities which it is busy imposing on defendants, that lawyers have failed to notice that it is just as possible and often much easier, for accident victims to cover themselves by their own first party insurance policies. Too often, legal argument (and we may add, legal education) has proceeded on the assumption that if an injured plaintiff fails to obtain damages, he will be left penniless. Had lawyers appreciated earlier that alternative methods of compensation are often available to accident victims, the whole development of liability rules might have been different. Indeed it is surely not too much to say that the huge growth of legal liability for personal injuries has itself powerfully inhibited the development of first party insurance against injury risks – even though that would be a much better way for these risks to be covered.

There may be other factors too, but enough has been said to show that the mess we are in today is not the result of one simple explanation. Social and legal problems like this often grow up almost accidentally, over long periods of time, which is what has happened here. But the system is a mess for all that.

7. DOES THE SYSTEM HAVE NON-COMPENSATORY BENEFITS?

IN the last chapter we suggested that the present law is unjust and inefficient as a compensation system. We now need to ask whether it may nevertheless have value in other ways. One of the surprising things about the present law is that the judges insist it is only designed as a compensation system, but the moment anyone proposes that it should be abolished and replaced by a better compensation system, then it is argued that, after all, the system has value as a deterrent or for other similar purposes. We shall now subject this claim to scrutiny.

PUNISHMENT AND DETERRENCE

Punishment

We have seen that the judges insist that the purpose of a claim for damages is compensation and not punishment. So the way in which the damages are calculated has all to do with what the plaintiff has lost or suffered, and has nothing to do with how badly the defendant has behaved. Provided that the basic threshold of negligence is passed the plaintiff recovers in full – the damages are not increased where the defendant has behaved very badly, nor are they reduced because the defendant was trying his best and only just fell below the law's requirements. There are some exceptions to this principle, where punitive or exemplary damages can be awarded, and these damages are avowedly fixed at a higher level in order to punish and deter; as we have noted, claims against the police for wrongful arrest and similar claims, may fall into this category. But punitive damages cannot be recovered in most ordinary actions for damages for injuries received in accidents.

It seems very likely that the public perception of the purposes of claims for damages differs on this point from the law as laid down by the judges. To go by media comments, many people seem to feel that damages ought to be awarded as a form of punishment for wrongdoing, and they often appear to be outraged by what appear to be low awards of damages where a plaintiff has not suffered substantial losses, or where the damages are fixed at the relatively low figure of £7,500 in cases of bereavement. Many lawyers would insist that this public attitude tends to confuse the two questions of punishment and compensation, and that there are good reasons for keeping them separate. For instance, the criminal law does not usually punish mere carelessness, but only intentional wrongdoing. Carelessness on the roads is an exception to this, and a driver can be prosecuted for driving without due care, but there are many other accidents which can occur in situations not constituting a crime at all. Most people would probably find it unreasonable for the criminal law to be invoked where accidents occur due to minor acts of carelessness – but civil liability does exist in many such cases. Then again, where there is some uncertainty about what happened, the criminal law requires proof beyond reasonable doubt, because it is a very serious matter to condemn a person as a criminal, and perhaps jail him for several years, and it would be unacceptable to do that unless we feel quite sure that he is guilty. But in the civil law, where punishment is not in question, a lower standard of proof prevails – it is only necessary to show that the complainant's story is more probable than not. This is called proof on the balance of probabilities and it may be of special importance where an accident has occurred, but witnesses are few.

Now that we have seen how damages are actually paid in most compensation cases, we can appreciate another very important reason for not using these cases as opportunities to punish the defendant. For we have seen that the actual wrongdoer hardly ever pays the damages. So the award of damages is not going to punish him anyhow. He may even be dead, but damages can still be awarded against his estate, and paid by his third party insurer. Even when damages are awarded against a company, and we think the company is somehow to blame as a corporate entity, the damages are still not going to hurt the actual people responsible. We have also seen the absurd way in which this fact is disregarded when heavy punitive damages are awarded against the police for a bad case of wrongful arrest, and once again the damages are paid by the public and not the actual officers responsible.

So we need to be careful when we think about the fairness or justice of the law in civil liability cases – it is pointless to urge that compensation should be paid *because* someone has done something wrong, and he deserves to be punished. One reason why the law of civil liability has got so out of control is probably because of public desires for vengeance against those thought to be responsible for serious accidents and injuries. This desire for vengeance may or may not be a good thing, but it is misdirected when it leads to demands for more compensation in more cases.

Unfortunately, the present system may also mislead the public into believing that when a substantial award of damages is being made, justice has been done against the wrongdoer. In other words, the public desire for vengeance may not only lead to demands for too much compensation, it may also lead to a real neglect of procedures for the punishment of people who should be punished. Precisely because the whole emphasis of the law is on compensation, it seems to distract attention from the possibility of actually punishing the guilty parties. Too often, cases of negligence occur in which some individuals, whether they are themselves defendants, or (more usually) employees or officials of a company or public body, appear to have been very seriously at fault – yet nothing is done to punish them. Only in the most extreme cases of gross negligence, for instance, are manslaughter charges ever brought in the case of a fatal accident. Only in the case of road accidents is it common practice to prosecute for lesser offences such as careless driving or reckless driving. In fact the criminal law does not have any general offence of carelessly or even recklessly endangering the life or safety of others, an omission which can only be explained by the mistaken belief that such cases can be taken care of by the law of civil liability. Such an offence is needed.

Deterrence

If the law is not designed to punish, is it of any value as a deterrent? Some people think it is. They believe that companies and public bodies can be deterred from committing negligent acts if they are threatened with liability for damages. There may be some areas of activity where the law of negligence has a minor deterrent effect, but in general, it seems unlikely that much of value would be lost if it were got rid of.

Certainly we can dismiss the idea that the law of negligence is a useful deterrent in the case of road accidents. Drivers on the road are already faced with a battery of criminal sanctions if they drive carelessly or dangerously. They can be fined or in extreme cases jailed. They can lose their licences. They can also be injured themselves if they drive badly. If all these things don't deter many people from bad driving it is absurd to think that they will be deterred by the thought that their insurance companies may have to pay a damages claim.

This does not necessarily prove that companies and public bodies cannot be deterred by the threat of legal liability,

but at least in the case of personal injuries, it seems probable that there are already plenty of other reasons why any
sensible company or public body will wish to avoid carelessly injuring its workers, or the public. Quite apart from
the sheer inhumanity of deliberately taking risks with life
or limb, most companies will find themselves subject to
financial penalties (and the ensuing bad publicity) for causing such injuries. There are so many safety regulations protecting workers from industrial injury that it must be rare
for an injury to occur without the breach of a regulation
somewhere. Any such breach makes companies liable to be
fined, although it is true that prosecutions are frequently
not brought for simple accidents unless there was indeed
some gross fault somewhere. Then again, any sensible
company knows that accidents cause other financial losses
quite apart from legal liability – indeed, there is research
suggesting that these other losses are likely to exceed any
damages payable. These losses stem from the disruption
produced in any organisation by an accident – conveyor
belts may need to be stopped in a factory, mining shafts
closed in a mine, even offices may need temporary closure
in the event of a serious accident. All these things will cost
money and no well-run company will lightly run the risk
of such losses even if they cynically disregard the safety of
their workforce or members of the public.

Besides, as we have already seen at some length, even
companies don't actually pay damages in most cases. It is
the insurers who pay. But then – some people have suggested – the insurer may charge higher premiums for those
who have bad accident records, so in this way, even insurance does not prevent legal liability from having a deterrent value in the long run. This is an interesting and
ingenious suggestion, but detailed research does not bear it
out. The subject is quite complicated, but the essential
point is that insurers cannot and do not vary premiums
very much according to accident record. It is too complex,

and too unreliable statistically. You can't assume that a company which had two or three accidents one year (when the industry average is only one accident per year) is necessarily a badly run company which is likely to have more accidents than the average next year. It may just be a statistical quirk – when you deal in large numbers, as insurers always do, statistical quirks are themselves of quite frequent occurrence, and have to be recognised for what they are.

There is another problem about relying on the law of damages as a deterrent – nobody is ever quite sure that it may not over deter in some situations. For instance, if doctors get paranoid about the threat of being sued (as many American doctors are) a tendency develops for the doctors to practise what the Americans have christened "defensive medicine". That means that the doctors start ordering a huge number of tests and X-rays on their patients, which are not medically justified, but which may protect the doctors if somebody later sues them. Now these tests and X-rays may not only be wasteful (it has been estimated that over one billion dollars annually is spent on unnecessary X-rays in America), they may actually carry some risks for the patients. Exposing a patient to an X-ray increases by a tiny amount the risk of certain cancers. Obviously if a few million unnecessary X-rays are being taken every year, it is likely that a few unnecessary cancers are going to develop. But nobody can sue for that because it will never be known who are the cancer patients who owe their cancers to unnecessary X-rays. In this way, liability for negligence can actually cause more harm than it prevents. (If anybody suggests that there is an inconsistency between the argument in this paragraph and the previous argument suggesting that liability does not deter at all in most cases, it must be remembered that damages are vastly higher in America, and that consequently some insurance premiums – such as those paid by many doctors – are simply enormous by English standards; what is more these premiums do vary or can vary according to the doctor's record. This does not yet happen in England.)

The fear of a kind of over-deterrence has influenced the judges in England in some cases where they have refused to hold some public bodies liable, such as in cases where it has been alleged that the police are responsible for a murder because they failed to arrest the murderer. In cases like this, liability for negligence might lead the police authorities to deploy their limited resources to try to minimise the risk of being sued, possibly against their better judgment, and against the public interest. This is a good reason for not imposing liability in these cases, and some of these judicial decisions are therefore to be welcomed.

On the whole, then, it seems doubtful if liability for negligence operates as a useful deterrence, and little would be lost by getting rid of it. There may be a few activities where special considerations arise, and these may need special treatment if the law is to be substantially revised. But the problem does not appear to be an extensive one.

ECONOMIC CONSIDERATIONS

In the past thirty years a huge literature has been spawned in America by a completely new "school" of law-and-economics scholars. This literature began with study of the accident-deterrence problem, and is therefore of some importance to us. What these scholars argued was somewhat complex and refined, though the basic idea is not really too difficult to grasp. This basic idea is that making people pay for the accidents they cause is not so much a deterrent to particular accidents, but is a way of persuading them to spend the appropriate levels of money on safety.

Suppose, for instance, a company is held liable for injuries caused by negligence on the roads, we cannot expect that this will do much to deter particular accidents. But we can perhaps expect that road haulage companies, or bus companies, will take more trouble over the selection and training of their drivers and the maintenance of their vehicles. Suppose a very large company finds itself regularly paying out a million pounds in damages for road accidents every year. They have an economic incentive to spend a lot of money in trying to reduce that figure. Suppose they can reduce their liability to half a million pounds a year by spending £200,000 on driver training and better maintenance. Clearly if they can do that, they will save overall £300,000 a year – and at the same time reduce the number of accidents. The theory is sometimes called the theory of "economic deterrence" or "market deterrence" to distinguish it from the simpler idea of deterrence by more direct means.

Some people will have a rooted objection to this kind of argument because they will feel that nobody should be allowed to weigh safety against cost considerations. Business activities (they may feel) should be as safe as they can be humanly made, not as safe as companies can afford. This is a widely held viewpoint but it is simply wrong. Safety and risk is *always* a relative matter. There is never such a thing as absolute safety. There are lots of accidents which could be prevented in society if we were prepared to pay the price. We could abolish all road accidents overnight by forbidding all motor traffic, for instance. There is no doubt that this solution would work but we don't do it because it would cost far too much – not just in terms of pounds, but in terms of what we should have to give up. And the same is true of all activities in which humans engage.

So the question always becomes, how much should be spent on safety, and the answer of these law-and-economics theorists is that companies should be left to make their own decisions about levels of safety expenditures, but they must realise that if they spend too little it will cost them more in the end because of the damages they will have to pay.

The theory depends for its soundness on the assumption that accidents have a "true" or "real" cost, and that damages represent that true cost. If this is not the case then companies who have to pay damages may be paying too little or too much, and either way the incentive to invest in the right levels of safety precautions will be distorted.

This book is not the place for any detailed assessment of the value of this theory. All that we need to say is that it has very little utility in the real world for a host of reasons. First, as we have emphasised over and over again, companies (like individuals) do not pay the damages in these cases; they are paid by insurers. The theorists respond with the argument we have already noted, that insurers can vary their premiums to suit the track record of individual insured parties. But this too we have seen is a very theoretical argument. It is in practice just not true that most companies will find their premiums significantly altered because of their accident record. Only with very large companies does this happen to any real degree. Eighty percent of companies are probably too small to be individually rated by insurers, who just lump most clients into groups, and assess them accordingly.

Then there is another problem about the assumption that companies are motivated by long-term financial calculations of the kind presupposed by this theory. Companies should perhaps be so motivated, but companies are run by real live managers and directors who may be motivated by other more short-term considerations. Lots of the serious liabilities encountered in the modern world (industrial diseases, pollution and so on) have long latency periods, that is to say, the companies whose activities may involve liabilities of this kind may be free from any problem for twenty or thirty years – so the current managers can expect to be retired or to have moved on long before then. So if it is just economic considerations which motivate them, then they are unlikely to worry about these long term liabilities, although the company as an entity will have to face the liabilities eventually.

Another reason why this theory need not be taken too seriously is that practically all activities which have some injury potential are regulated in all sorts of ways in the modern world. Licensing, testing, inspections, supervision, and criminal prosecution are all alternative methods of trying to control the levels of safety that a society may insist upon. So long as this array of controls remains in place it hardly matters whether a company operates under some kind of economic deterrence. What is more, there are many activities in which a company's reputation (and hence profits) are far more likely to motivate its behaviour than its legal liabilities. A food company, for instance, which sells tainted meat and causes an outbreak of E-coli, may well be liable to pay damages to its customers who are made ill, but it can hardly be supposed that food companies would not do their utmost to avoid this kind of thing even if they were not liable to pay these damages. So long as the public health authorities have the power to investigate, and if necessary, close down businesses who are causing such an outbreak, the liability to pay damages seems completely unnecessary as a deterrent, or even as an economic incentive.

We are left at the end with a residual argument which needs perhaps to be borne in mind. This argument basically is that activities of different kinds should not be subsidised by other activities but should bear their own costs. Where possible, road transport should bear the cost of road traffic accidents; railway transport should bear the cost of railway accidents; air traffic should bear the cost of aircraft accidents; shipping transport should bear the cost of shipping accidents; and so on. If we can structure our compensation laws to achieve this result, by all means let us do so, but the theory is too impractical to justify distorting our personal injury compensation system in order to try to meet it.

These economic arguments may have more weight in certain kinds of property damage cases, (for example, in shipping accidents) and in that context we may need to keep them in mind.

PUBLIC ACCOUNTABILITY

It is sometimes urged that the right to bring an action for damages is a useful way of making large institutions, public or even private, more publicly accountable for their behaviour. Suppose a child goes into hospital for a minor operation or some, apparently not very serious, disease. If the child suddenly dies, the parents will be greatly shocked, and suffer severe anguish. They may also find that it is hard to discover exactly what has happened, why the death occurred, and all their inquiries may be fobbed off. If that happens, they may take comfort from the fact that by bringing an action for damages they may be able to bring the issues into the open and force the hospital authorities to come to court and give evidence, where their barrister can cross-examine them and try to get at the truth. In this way the action for damages may serve a sort of inquisitorial purpose – the purpose may not be so much to obtain compensation but to ask questions and get answers.

Or again, take a case which has been much discussed in the media while these pages were being written, the claim for damages for bullying at school which was apparently settled by a payment of £30,000 in damages. Some people may feel dubious about the idea that such a huge sum should be paid in compensation for mere bullying (though I have pointed out earlier that the settlement must have been based on the assumption that the victim was severely traumatized and hence unable to work for some time in consequence); but others may think that the ability to claim damages in this way has served a useful purpose by bringing the issue to public attention. One newspaper, indeed, has proclaimed that the case has put bullying at the top of the agenda for schools.

There is something in these claims that a legal action can have a useful function as a sort of inquiry mechanism in some cases. But unfortunately the action for damages is very ill-suited for this purpose, and in general probably does more harm than good. For one thing, as we have repeatedly stressed, the purpose of a claim for damages is compensatory. The law is geared to that purpose in a variety of ways. For instance, suppose that there is indeed reason for public disquiet over the behaviour of some public body like a hospital, as in the hypothetical example above. There may well be a real public need for an open inquiry into what has happened, to allay public anxieties, but if someone issues a writ claiming damages against the hospital, a public inquiry is quite probably the last thing that will happen. First, everyone will clam up even more than before because the insurers (if any, or the lawyers, if none) will instruct the hospital staff not to talk about the issues at all. Secondly, if there really is anything discreditable the hospital wishes to conceal it will certainly make a substantial offer to settle the case. Because of the rules about costs discussed in Chapter 1, (above, p. 23) this means that the complainant can only reject the offer and proceed with his lawsuit if he is willing to run the risk of a huge bill for costs at the end. And even if he is so willing, where he is on legal aid, the legal aid authorities will probably withdraw their financial assistance. The case will not then proceed at all. In other words, precisely *because* the main purpose of the law is to compensate the injured, a public inquiry which it may be in the public interest to hold, will not actually be held. The fact that Pan-American Airways (or its insurers) has settled most of the claims of the victims of the Lockerbie air disaster is perhaps illustrative. These claims were, apparently, based on the suggestion that Pan-Am had prior knowledge of a possible bomb threat which it chose to ignore. One might have thought it was in the public interest that the facts about this allegation should have been fully and publicly investigated – after all the *scientific* causes of an air crash are always investigated by public agencies. But the facts about the alleged prior knowledge have never been publicly investigated, and to this day the world does not know the whole truth about the allegations. Settling the damages claims has disposed of the allegations.

But even in cases where a trial does go ahead, although it is undeniable that in some cases this may lead to a useful public airing of important issues, there are other respects in which this is quite an inappropriate setting for this kind of inquiry. In a claim for damages the whole focus of attention is on the plaintiff's complaint, and on the reasonableness of the defendant's conduct as regards that particular plaintiff. But it is often impossible to judge the reasonableness of that conduct except in a wider context which would require the court to embark on a far broader inquiry. Take the case of the school-bullying claim, mentioned above. As already said, some people think this case served a useful purpose in putting bullying at the top of the agenda for schools, even though this case was settled and no trial was held. But anyhow, why *should* bullying be at the top of the agenda? Schools have many problems on their agenda – dilapidated buildings, class sizes, the quality of the teaching, the need for new equipment like computers, school truancy, examination results, and so on. The list is endless, and head teachers, school governors and local education authorities are responsible for adopting a balanced approach to these problems, and deciding which should be at the top of the agenda, and which should have a lower priority. If a parent or a child can put bullying at the top of the agenda by issuing a writ claiming damages, he is in effect jumping the queue; we are allowing him, rather than the proper authorities, to decide what should be at the top of the agenda. So this is not necessarily such a good idea after all.

In many really serious cases where disasters have occurred or especially terrible events have taken place, public inquiries *are* held, but they are ordered by ministers or the government, or sometimes by local authorities, and their job is to ascertain the facts and make recommendations. These inquiries are often held by judges or senior barristers and closely resemble trials for damages – except that their purpose is not to award damages to anybody. They are actually much better instruments than actions for damages for these purposes. All the same, it cannot be denied that in some cases there is a need for a procedure which an individual citizen can use, to demand an inquiry about some problem, or some event, and if there is no right to sue, a weapon will be lost which, if not the most suitable, still does have some use in certain contexts. The answer to this problem must lie elsewhere. Perhaps it lies in a Freedom of Information Act which enables the citizen to get at information controlled by public agencies. Or perhaps it should be made possible for citizens to initiate an inquiry in certain cases, of their own motion; or, (in the case of schools) the answer may lie in greater use of Ombudsmen. There are already many Ombudsmen who are able to inquire into individual grievances against public bodies like hospitals (such as the National Health Ombudsman) and their inquiries cost the complainant nothing. Perhaps we also need Ombudsmen for schools. Perhaps local councillors should be more aware of their role as representatives of their electors (like MPs) and hold local "surgeries" at which public issues can be raised. This book is not designed to suggest reforms to the whole political system so the matter cannot be pursued here. All that needs to be said here is that the problem is not best dealt with by litigation.

8. WHAT CAN WE DO ABOUT IT?

THIS book has covered a wide range of different kinds of claims for damages, and if there is one overall message that comes through, it is that the whole system of legal liability needs a good hard look. Unfortunately, there is really nobody capable of giving it the look it needs. The main difficulty is that the subject is far too important to be entrusted solely to lawyers, but nobody else understands it well enough to be able to propose the deep-rooted reforms really required. The one body which might have been able to do this job – the Law Commission – is far too closely wedded to the system and its underlying value structure, to be able to bring to bear the independent scrutiny the system needs. In the long run the only solution to the difficulty must lie in educating the public to understand more fully the nature of the system we live under, and who pays its costs. Perhaps lawyers too need educating, because though they may understand the nuts and bolts of the system, they do not see it in full perspective. In particular, lawyers know very little about cases where legal claims are not normally made.

But readers of this book may feel they are entitled to something more concrete in the way of suggestions for improvement, and the remainder of this chapter will therefore take up this challenge. It is divided into three parts. In the first part a few proposals are made which extend over much of the field of civil liability. In the second and third parts the emphasis will be on actions for damages for various kinds of personal injuries, including claims arising from fatal accidents.

A NEW LOOK AT THE WHOLE SYSTEM OF CIVIL LIABILITY

Obviously, in a book of this nature, we can only make a few tentative suggestions about such an extensive subject as reforming the whole system of civil liability, but a number of salient points do emerge from the first seven chapters in this book.

First, the law must reflect the fact that in the great majority of cases damages are not paid by individual wrongdoers but by insurance companies or other large bodies. The consequences of this need to be faced. For one thing individual wrongdoers get off too lightly at present. The law of damages makes no serious effort to punish those who are guilty of causing serious injury or loss to others – and by those who are guilty, I mean the actual, responsible parties, not employers or public bodies or insurance companies. While nobody would want to institute witch-hunts against those who are guilty of nothing more than minor acts of carelessness, far too many people get away with much more serious wrongdoing for which they are neither punished by the law nor even disciplined by their employers, or their professional bodies. A new criminal offence of recklessly endangering members of the public needs to be created, which should operate across the board and not just deal with driving offences. The disciplining of employees and professionals guilty of really serious fault, gross carelessness or recklessness, also need to be taken much more seriously, whether the consequences are physical injury or merely financial or other losses.

Next, the law of vicarious and corporate and public responsibility needs to be comprehensively reviewed. Punitive damages should be abolished in cases of vicarious liability – it is contrary to all principle to punish one person for the misdeeds of another, and it serves no useful purpose to do so. Even ordinary civil liability for compensatory damages needs to be given a long hard look where the defendant is a corporation or a public body. Every kind of claim for damages should be scrutinised to see if it arises from circumstances where it is more appropriate for the plaintiff or the defendant to cover the risk by insurance. Certainly, liability for causing property damage by fire could be abolished in the case of insured property, which is another way of saying that the doctrine of subrogation should be abolished in these cases, and possibly in others too. This is one reform which could at a single blow simplify the law, and save the public money as well.

Liability for personal injury is dealt with more fully again below, so the main question to be considered here is how far corporations or public bodies should be held civilly liable for economic losses and new forms of injury or loss which do not fall into the traditional categories of personal injury or property damage. An inquiry of this kind cannot be limited to the law of negligence, but must take into account the law of contract as well. To pursue this in any detail would take us into areas well beyond the scope of this book, but we have seen examples of cases (such as the claims of photographers for loss of their films, above, p. 136) where the present law permits claims to be made which are contrary to the general interests of consumers. These sorts of claims should also be abolished, though abolition should be combined with new facilities for protection of the consumer by insurance, as already suggested (p. 137).

The liability of accountants and other professionals for unlimited sums in cases of financial loss should also be abolished. As this proposal is unlikely to command general agreement, a reasonable holding reform would be to limit the liability of such firms to some overall figure likely to be within the current limits of their insurance cover. Certainly, if nothing is done about this type of liability it can only be a matter of time before a large firm of accountants is bankrupted and completely broken up by some enormous legal claim. That will lead to some serious government inquiry and the law will then be changed. But wouldn't it be more sensible for once to introduce a reform before a major failure of the system actually occurs?

Over and beyond these specific proposals it is highly desirable to shift the law away from the strongly paternalist ideology which has influenced it for some decades. As we have seen, paternalism underlies much of the blame culture; it encourages people to see others as responsible for taking precautions against accidents and injuries, and also as responsible for protecting them by insurance or other means, when misfortune does strike. The messages sent by this sort of paternalist ideology are little short of disastrous, and are closely linked to the culture of the welfare state in its heyday – the idea that the state would be responsible for caring for its citizens "from the cradle to the grave". It may well be, in fact, that it is the gradual collapse of this welfare state ideal which is driving so much of the litigation process today. People who have grown up believing that the state would always look after them, no matter what misfortunes should strike, are now driven to find someone to sue, when they discover that the state will not and cannot deliver on this expectation. Litigation is clearly no real solution to these problems from society's viewpoint, though it may be a solution for a small number of successful plaintiffs. The only real solution to these problems in the long run is the spread of more first party insurance.

Even where paternalism is genuinely necessary, because society is taking on itself the care of those who are unable to care for themselves, because they are (for instance) children in care, or mental patients, we need to be extremely careful to distinguish between our desire to render assistance to those who need it, and any duty to pay compensation where we fail. In this respect the law is at present on the right track, though under challenge in the European Court of Human Rights.

PERSONAL INJURIES: SOME DEAD ENDS

We turn now to consider possible reforms to the system of compensation for personal injuries and fatal accidents, and this must be done at somewhat greater length, both because of its intrinsic importance, and because the subject has been very much debated for many years and in many countries.

We have seen that most damage awards are paid by insurance companies, and that it is insurance companies who actually handle and administer virtually the whole system. Of course they do this under the supervision of the courts, and anybody who thinks he is getting an unfair deal from an insurer can try "appealing", as it were, to the courts. Although some public bodies, like the central government (the Crown) and perhaps also a very few private bodies do not insure, this does not alter the general position.

Now this means that the system we have is in reality an insurance system, and we need to treat it as such. If you have an insurance policy and you find that it does not afford you the sort of coverage you would like, and costs too much, the natural reaction is that you should change your insurance policy for one with wider coverage and lower costs. So also if society as a whole finds that the insurance system it has offers too limited a coverage and costs too much, society needs to change its insurance system.

Let us first try to recap briefly about this insurance system which we can treat as the equivalent of an actual policy. The "policy" or system gives you cover against the risks of being injured (or it gives your dependants cover if you are killed) in an accident which can be proved to be someone else's fault. If you are covered, then the benefits are very generous indeed; and although they may be welcomed in serious cases, they are, frankly, often over-generous in minor ones. Do you really want insurance coverage against the risk of a few scratches and minor abrasions and would you still want it if you had to pay separately for it? So, some of the benefits may be too large, but on the other hand, the coverage is minuscule compared to the ordinary risks of life. Virtually no coverage for illness, or death from natural causes; practically no coverage for birth defects which may affect your children, and even in the case of accidental injury the coverage is very limited. Coverage for road accidents is fairly good, but even then only extends to about a quarter of road accident victims, or a little more. But taking all accidents into consideration, the coverage is hopelessly inadequate. If you are an accident victim your chances of recovering damages are less than one in ten; and if you are disabled from other causes, perhaps only one or two in a hundred. For this fragmented and limited coverage you pay a pretty stiff premium in the form of a third party motor premium plus a levy on all the goods and services you buy. This policy is just not good enough. If you had an insurance broker and asked him to find you a policy to cover you against the risk of accident or injury, and this was the best he could come up with, you would hardly believe him.

So what can we do about it? We will first explore some proposals which turn out to be dead ends, and will then go on to outline some more promising proposals.

First possible reform: cover everybody with damages levels of compensation

Since compensation for those who *are* covered by the present "policy" or system looks fine, indeed very generous, perhaps the first solution that may come to mind is simply to extend this coverage to all accident victims and all victims of handicaps and disabilities arising from natural causes. Alas, it only takes a moment's study of the figures to show that this solution is totally impossible. Given our rough estimate that about one billion pounds is today spent on damages, plus another £800 million on administering the system, and given that all this largesse goes on only one and a half percent of all injured or handicapped people, it is easy to see that extending the system to everybody would result in a compensation bill in the region of £66 billion a year, plus administrative costs. Even though the costs would be greatly reduced (proportionately speaking) because they would be much lower in a universal scheme, they could hardly be much less than ten or twelve percent of the sums disbursed – say a total round figure of £75 billion annually for compensation and administrative costs. That figure is close to the total cost of the *entire* social security budget today, and is not far short of a quarter of all government expenditure. So a compensation system of this kind would involve an immense increase in taxation, and would also pre-empt probably all future increases on other government services like schools, the NHS, law and order and so on, for generations to come. Plainly this is just not a serious proposition.

But if there is no possibility of handing out tort levels of damages to all handicapped and injured victims, continuous "stretching" of the tort system is pretty pointless. As we saw earlier (p. 32) it just amounts to squeezing one or two percent more victims into the privileged class who receive the bonanza of damages, while leaving less and less money available for all the others.

Second possible reform: leave the present compensation system alone but gradually increase benefits for others

This is, roughly speaking, the policy which was adopted in the 1960s and 1970s. Damages levels were not reduced (indeed they may have increased) but other victims of injury and disability were offered gradually improved benefits under the social security system and the other benefits of the welfare state. In some respects these benefits began to become quite valuable, especially for long-term and permanent incapacities. Although the social security system has never handed out huge lump sums like the law of damages, pensions payable over a life time can actually have a considerable total value; and some of the benefits of the welfare state (such as pensions payable for permanent and severe industrial injuries) do actually have a real value not far short of the levels of damages in certain cases. So this was a policy of levelling-up, as it were, though for the reasons given above, it was always clear that the levelling up could not possibly continue until some sort of parity was achieved.

Unfortunately, even the levelling-up has ceased in recent years. Social security spending has stopped rising so steeply as it was doing twenty years ago, and indeed, for the last few years it has actually fallen. The government is constantly struggling to whittle down the social security budget which already consumes something like a quarter of all taxes, and there seems no likelihood that even the election of a Labour Government will make a great deal of difference. Indeed, there are many signs that future governments will try to persuade the public to take on themselves the responsibility for insuring against more and more of the risks covered by social security at present. Furthermore, damages awards appear to be increasing too, so the gap between the compensation awarded to the privileged few and the unlucky many is today probably wider than ever, and likely to widen still further. So there seems no future in this kind of reform.

Third possible reform: a national accident compensation plan

During the 1960s great interest was aroused throughout the world by the bold and dramatic Woodhouse Report in

New Zealand. In 1967 Mr Justice Woodhouse proposed in a detailed and highly persuasive report that all liability for damages for accidental personal injuries should be abolished; and should be replaced by a national accident compensation scheme. Under this scheme a State Board would basically take over the job of insuring everyone against personal injury caused by any kind of accident. The compensation offered was nothing like as generous as the damages awarded in legal suits, but it was not niggardly either. Every person who lost earnings was to receive approximately 80 per cent of his losses in compensation (up to a pre-set ceiling), and some other pecuniary losses could also be covered, especially in very serious cases, such as payments to adapt a home to make it suitable for a disabled person, or even to adapt a car for the same purpose. Medical expenses were also to be covered. There would be no compensation for pain and suffering though the Report did not wholly rule out some small payments for loss of amenities in very serious cases.

The most remarkable thing about the Report was its estimate that all these benefits could be provided at a cost which barely exceeded the existing cost of the compensation paid under the damages system. It could be funded relatively easily by levies on motorists, replacing the existing third party premiums, and levies on employers, replacing the amounts they already paid for employers' liability insurance.

After many years of detailed discussion and further debate a version of the Woodhouse scheme was implemented by the New Zealand Parliament in 1972. This far-reaching reform was hailed by many as showing the way ahead for the UK, and pressure mounted for the appointment of a Royal Commission to inquire into the problem in this country. After the thalidomide tragedy in which hundreds of grossly disabled and deformed babies were born to mothers who had been prescribed the drug thalidomide, and the public discovered that many claims for damages on behalf of these babies were still unsettled ten years after the events, a Royal Commission was eventually set up under Lord Pearson. This Royal Commission, however, did not follow the path blazed by Mr Justice Woodhouse. It produced hundreds of minor recommendations, but could not agree on abolition of the action for damages, nor indeed was it agreed on any basic idea or philosophy which could have underpinned its own recommendations. It did produce a mass of facts and statistics (which have been extensively used and quoted in this book) but eventually the Report was largely discarded. Although there are many academic lawyers who still believe that a national accident compensation scheme is the answer to the problem, any such scheme looks today increasingly unlikely. This kind of reform is considered further in the next section for reasons which will become apparent.

Fourth possible reform: an all-embracing national compensation plan

Although the Woodhouse Report and the ensuing New Zealand legislation did have many attractions, there were niggling doubts. One major doubt concerned the fact that the Report and the legislation did nothing for the victims of birth defects or handicaps and disabilities arising from natural causes. So in a sense the Report greatly enlarged the number of the privileged beneficiaries, but still did not tackle the underlying inequity. A man who seriously injured himself falling off a ladder while painting his house could now get compensation, (which he still cannot do in Britain) but a man who had his leg removed by a surgeon because it was diseased could not. Mr Justice Woodhouse himself had made it clear that he saw no reason why the principles he had laid down should not be extended to all disabilities and handicaps, and in 1972 he was invited by the newly-elected Australian Labor government to come to Australia and head a small committee to produce recommendations for that country. (The present writer, who was at that time teaching at the Australian National University, was a member of this committee but left Australia before the Report was presented.)

The Australian Woodhouse committee produced a two-part set of recommendations. The first part was broadly similar to the New Zealand proposals; but the second part was an even more far-reaching set of proposals to extend the accident scheme, with some modifications, to all disabilities and handicaps and birth defects arising from natural causes. This gigantic social welfare scheme was estimated to cost something like four times as much as the basic accident compensation scheme, which though a pretty massive expenditure, was not by any means an impossible one for a modern state. But neither part of the Australian committee proposals was ever implemented. Detailed inquiries before the Australian parliament dragged on for some years, eventually the Labor government fell and was replaced by a much more conservative government, and the proposals were shelved.

Despite their utopian qualities, the Woodhouse schemes no longer seem as attractive as they were twenty years ago. Both involve massive bureaucratic extensions of the welfare state of a kind which have gone out of fashion with governments and electorates. And they have gone out of fashion not just because of normal swings of public opinion, but because experience of similar bureaucratic schemes has been uniformly unsatisfactory in the modern world. They have proved unsatisfactory for a number of reasons. First, their cost estimates nearly always prove to have been too optimistic, as indeed has happened in New Zealand where their legislation has recently been cut down partly for reasons of cost. This is often because inadequate allowance is made for the way that generous compensation schemes actually alter human behaviour. Those who are entitled to accident sick pay of eighty percent of their normal pay will often feel that they are almost as well off resting at home after an accident than getting back to work. Pre-legislation data about the length of time that workers take off after certain kinds of injury may thus prove unreliable after such a scheme is introduced. A second problem is that massive new schemes of this kind invariably throw up anomalies and inconsistencies of treatment which require amendment; the tendency then is to make amendments which are still more favourable to the victims, and add further to costs. A third problem is that schemes of this kind often prove too rigid. They involve imposing the same solution on many different problems, the same benefits to people in many different situations. In short they lack the flexibility of market solutions.

A fourth problem, especially with truly enormous social schemes like the second part of the Woodhouse Australian committee proposals, is that they do seem to have an effect not unlike that of the "blame culture". While they may not actually encourage the public to blame others for their misfortunes, they certainly encourage the public to think that it is someone else's responsibility to pick up the pieces after a misfortune has occurred. These are of course politically controversial questions, and it is not possible to assess them fully in a book like this; but undoubtedly the current mood in most Western countries is hostile to the idea that it should always be the job of government to sort things out when they go wrong.

It is also easy to see how every step taken by the government along these lines leads inexorably to demands for the next step. The Woodhouse accidents scheme leads to demands for a Woodhouse sickness and disease scheme. But where does this process stop? If all accidental deaths are to be covered by a national compensation scheme, are all deaths from disease to be so covered too? That means that the state would take over a substantial part of the life insurance industry. Do we really want that? Or again, if those who are widowed by accidental deaths are to receive generous compensation benefits, what about deserted wives? Aren't they treated today as in the same social category, with the same needs, as widows? And if deserted wives, what about single mothers? Or single fathers? Plainly, compensation schemes cannot take on board the state's entire social policy. That would be a case of the tail wagging the dog.

The Woodhouse schemes were visionary and courageous plans; but it seems unlikely that reform along these lines is really the answer to the problems of the twenty-first century. The one thing of lasting importance that emerges from the Woodhouse Reports is the demonstration that the existing system of damages for personal injuries is unfair and inefficient and can be abolished. Despite some scaling down of the New Zealand legislation, as noted above, the one thing that New Zealand has not turned its back upon since introducing its national compensation scheme is the decision to get rid of the damages action in its entirety.

THE WAY AHEAD: ROAD ACCIDENTS

In this and the final section some proposals are outlined which would go a long way to providing a more modern and rational system of compensation for accidents and injuries. We will start with road accidents.

Some countries, and many of the separate states or provinces in the US, Australia and Canada have already established special no-fault road accident compensation schemes. These vary widely, but they are all designed to compensate those injured in road accidents without the need to prove fault, and are based on the first party insurance principle. Coverage is therefore universal, or almost so (there are sometimes exclusions for people like "fleeing felons" or drunken drivers). Usually these schemes offer reasonable compensation for earnings losses and medical expenses, but nothing for pain and suffering. Sometimes they completely replace claims for damages; sometimes they offer benefits without depriving the victim of the right to sue, though in that case they all require deduction (or repayment) of the no-fault benefits from the damages recovered; in some American states the right to sue is only left intact for serious injuries. Sometimes the insurance is handled by private insurers in the same way that they handle the vehicle comprehensive insurance system; in other places the personal injury insurance is placed in the hands of a state board or authority of some kind.

Practically any one of these no-fault schemes would be better than what we currently have though by far the most successful schemes are those which completely abolish the right to sue for damages. They are cheaper to operate and provide much wider coverage; they are generally able to start paying compensation for earnings losses on a weekly or monthly basis much sooner than the present damages system. The costs do not fall on governments, but are easily met from levies on drivers (replacing existing third party premiums). The adversary relationship between the victim and the other party's insurer is eliminated and replaced by a relationship either with a first party insurer, or with a state authority which is not a money-making institution.

A road accident no-fault scheme, run by the private insurance industry, would actually be perfectly easy to introduce in this country. Because of the existing third party system, which is well known, and rigorously enforced, it would be quite straightforward to abolish legal liability for damages for accidents arising on the road, and simply replace it with a claim against your own insurer. (To insure universal coverage for road accidents it would be necessary to provide, as many schemes abroad already provide, that passengers and pedestrians, if not covered by their own policies, would be covered by the insurance over the vehicle involved in the accident.) Claims would generally be made in the same way you claim for damage to your vehicle under a comprehensive policy. If you suffer an injury with a consequent loss of earnings, the insurance company would doubtless require certificates from your doctor that you are unable to work, and a simple form from the employer giving your normal earnings, and weekly benefit payments could then be made very rapidly. There seems every likelihood that a scheme of this kind would cost no more than the existing system, with all its absurdities and inefficiencies and inadequate coverage, because of the huge savings that can be made on legal and administrative expenses by a no-fault scheme, and the elimination of payments for minor pain and suffering claims. Detailed research studies of several American no-fault schemes have confirmed this fact.

There might be theoretical arguments in favour of making such a new kind of insurance entirely voluntary, but too many people would probably end up without any cover if that were done. For purely pragmatic reasons, therefore, it would probably be necessary to make this kind of insurance compulsory, just like third party insurance, but there would still be very great advantages about switching to a first party insurance scheme. For one thing, it would be possible to limit the compulsory element of the policy, while allowing for optional extra coverage at additional premiums. Consider for instance, the size of the income-loss which should be covered by a first-party policy. There seems no reason at all why this should not be set at a fairly modest level – say £250 per week – so long as the insured has the option to extend the cover to much higher limits if he wants, and is prepared to pay the extra premium involved. At present, of course, the third party liability system means that there is no limit to the income loss which is recoverable if negligence is provable – so pop singers or tennis stars may be entitled to several million pounds for a few years' income loss (see p. 9), all of which naturally has to come from the sums paid by people whose income is very much lower. In a first party system, there is absolutely no reason to insist that everybody should insure against a high income loss if he doesn't have, and is unlikely ever to have, a high income. Indeed, for some people – pensioners, for instance – there is no very obvious reason why they should be compelled to insure against income loss at all. To make them do so would simply perpetuate one of the unfairnesses of the existing system. Similarly, motorists should be able to choose whether they want life insurance benefits under a first party policy. Many who have adequate life insurance of a more conventional kind would feel there was no point in buying extra life insurance to cover road accidents. Some motorists have no dependants and would not see any point in having life insurance at all. Others may choose to buy substantial life cover as an optional extra. Why should they all be compelled to buy it, as the third party system effectively compels them to do?

Other additional items of extra cover could no doubt be made available if there appears to be a market demand for them. If people really want some cover for non-pecuniary loss, for instance, insurers could doubtless offer this as an optional extra, but again there seems no reason why anybody should be forced to buy it. Possibly, though, some element of "catastrophe" cover should be compulsory – that is where truly appalling injuries are suffered in an accident which renders the victim a complete paraplegic or something of that kind. In cases like this there is evidently some real point to a particularly special level of cover regardless of financial loss.

THE WAY AHEAD: OTHER ACCIDENTS AND INJURIES

If a no-fault road accident scheme of this kind were established, what should be done about other accidents and injuries, and disabilities from other causes? It would not be so easy to replace the right to sue with first party insurance in any other kind of case, because we do not have such a widespread and readily understood kind of insurance, like the motor insurance system, which could simply be transformed into a first party system. It is true that there are limited fields, like workers' compensation or medical misadventures where special schemes could be established, and indeed have been established in some countries. But there would even then remain many accidents, like those occurring in the home, or in playing sports, or even in schools, which are uncovered by any no-fault schemes, and would remain subject to all the vagaries and inefficiencies of the action for damages.

There is only one really effective solution to this problem. The action for damages for personal injuries should simply be abolished, and first-party insurance should be left to the free market. This proposal may seem at first sight little short of revolutionary, but closer examination shows that it is a perfectly natural development of current trends.

For a start, it should not be assumed that the action for damages for personal injuries is in any sense a real cornerstone of our legal system. This type of legal liability is actually of quite recent origin in the history of modern legal systems. In fact it is little more than a century old, and its rise closely parallels the rise of third party liability insurance. In other words this kind of legal action, as a routine measure for income-loss coverage, has simply grown up in the modern world where insurance itself has become more and more common. Unfortunately, the law got onto the wrong track from the very outset, developing and encouraging third party insurance instead of first party insurance. So to abolish the action for damages for personal injuries today would only be to put the law back onto the right lines from which it diverged a hundred years ago. Many countries have already abolished the action for damages for

special kinds of injuries, such as road accidents and workers' compensation injuries. There is no evidence that this
causes any sense of grievance or public outrage, provided
that some kind of adequate alternative insurance system is
put in its place.

Nor is the detailed critique offered in this book against
the action for damages for personal injuries at all new. All
these criticisms have been made time and again in the past
thirty years, never more effectively than in the Woodhouse
Reports. The only thing that has really changed since those
Reports is that the state compensation systems proposed as
replacements for the action for damages now seem hopelessly dated. The criticisms of the action for damages itself
are still entirely valid. It is natural, therefore, to suggest
today that abolition should be followed by a replacement
more in accord with current and likely future trends. And
there seems no doubt − whatever the complexion of future
governments − that the trend in these matters is going to
be to require people to assume more and more responsibility for insuring themselves against the risks of life.

What is more, if the case for abolition of the present system is once agreed to be made out, the only really practical alternative today (except for road accidents) seems to be
to leave the matter largely to the free market. If we don't
do this, we shall probably end up with a whole collection
of special compensation schemes, one for road accidents,
one for workers' compensation, one perhaps for medical
injuries, one for sporting injuries and so on. The compensation payable for all these kinds of injuries will doubtless
differ from case to case, with just as many anomalies and
absurdities as we have today. Only if we allow people the
free choice to make their own decisions as to what kind of
insurance they want, will these variations become acceptable.

Of course a transitional period of several years would be
needed before such a change could be implemented, and

in the interim it would be necessary for the insurance industry, with pressure from the government, to come up with some sensible proposals for first-party insurance schemes to be established which would cover most of the ordinary forms of accident. People would in this way be encouraged to insure themselves and their families against these risks. No doubt this would not just be done on an individual policy basis – groups of people would be encouraged to take out policies together. For example, schools should take out policies to cover their children against sporting injuries on a no-fault basis (actually this is already beginning). Employers and trade unions should be encouraged to co-operate in taking out policies to cover the workers against industrial accidents. Homeowners' insurance policies should cover people against accidents in the home on a no-fault basis. Pregnant women should be encouraged to insure against the risk of having a disabled baby. And so on. Nobody can really predict how this would all work out because we have never really had a free market in this way, operating in a framework where there is no legal liability to damages. Once this kind of liability goes, and therefore third party insurance goes too, the insurance industry will surely come up with all kinds of new proposals for first party policies.

The most difficult problems undoubtedly centre round disabilities arising from natural diseases and conditions. The public simply are not used to insuring against these risks, yet to leave them uninsured means that nothing would be done, for instance, for the little girl who lost her legs as a result of meningitis, one of the stories with which we began this book. Somehow, some kind of insurance protection against these risks needs to be built into any new system – certainly the insurance industry needs to think hard about ways of advertising the desirability of of this sort of insurance protection; perhaps also the government should encourage people to take out insurance when their children are born, by offering to pay part of the cost. The problem is not easy, and ideas may need to be co-ordinated between the insurance industry, and the social services and social security agencies. But the basic point must be the gradual encouragement of first-party insurance by more and more people, with the state simply acting as a fall-back protection for those who have no insurance of their own.

There would be enormous advantages in this course. First, we should get rid of all the wasteful legal and administrative costs associated with claims for damages and third party insurance. The taxpayer will gain as much as the premium payer, because the Lord Chancellor will suddenly find he does not need so many judges, and the costs of legal aid will also be cut. And the government itself will no longer have to pay damages for personal injury and will be able to get rid of (or redeploy) many of the lawyers it currently employs to handle these cases. (Although lawyers will bitterly oppose these proposals, it is unlikely that the demand for legal services will fall very much in the long run – the additional demands being put on lawyers by our membership of the European Union is such that lawyers are likely to be in short supply for a generation.)

Secondly, it will vastly improve the coverage which most people have against a large variety of risks. Instead of being offered a small, often a minuscule, chance of recovering enormous damages for some injuries, people will have a much better chance of obtaining reasonable compensation for all, or anyhow, most injuries. What is more, the compensation will be obtainable on a much fairer basis than the present lottery – broadly, you will get what you choose to pay for.

Third, this reform would begin the job of getting rid of the artificial distinctions embodied in the present law and practice between accidental injuries and disabilities from other causes. Although this would not come anywhere near the wildly ambitious Australian Woodhouse proposal to cover all disabilities and sickness in the same way (more or less) as accidents, it would gradually begin the process of getting people to think about insuring themselves against disabilities which arise from non-accidental causes.

Fourth, the shift to a free market in insurance would introduce a great deal of consumer choice in an area where it is significantly absent today – as we have seen, it could enable people to decide what level of income they want to insure, whether they want life insurance and so on. For this reason, also, it will distribute more equitably the burden of many accidents, where at present the third party system favours the more highly paid and discriminates against the low-paid, the unemployed and the retired. It means that the right people would be paying for the insurance cover for their own possible income losses.

Sixthly, it will get rid of the adversarial process which can be especially troublesome in the case of claims against hospitals.

Some may object that this idea is all very well for those who can afford to insure themselves, but what about those who can't? But the answer to this is that almost everybody will actually save more money by abolishing the present system than they will need to pay for their new first party insurance. The poorest people, especially, will actually save on their motor insurance policies, which should become substantially cheaper for those on low incomes, or for the pensioners who don't need income-loss protection or life insurance cover. And even those who don't have cars will save on the price of goods and services, as businesses will no longer have to pay huge premiums to cover the risk of damages claims. Of course some state social security safety net will still be needed for those who are not otherwise covered at all.

This would indeed be a reform worth striving for.

INDEX